20 Strategies for Collaborative School Leaders

Jane Clark Lindle

EYE ON EDUCATION
6 DEPOT WAY WEST, SUITE 106
LARCHMONT, NY 10538
(914) 833-0551
(914) 833-0761 fax
www.eyeoneducation.com

Copyright © 2005 Eye On Education, Inc.
All Rights Reserved.

For information about permission to reproduce selections from this book, write: Eye On Education, Permissions Dept., 6 Depot Way West, Suite 106, Larchmont, NY 10538.

Library of Congress Cataloging-in-Publication Data

Lindle, Jane Clark.
　20 strategies for collaborative school leaders / Jane Clark Lindle.
　　p. cm.
　ISBN 1-59667-000-2
　1. School management and organization—United States. 2. Educational leadership—United States. I. Title: Twenty strategies for collaborative school leaders. II. Title.
　LB2805.L49 2005
　　371.2—dc22

2004030425

Editorial services and production provided by
UB Communications, 10 Lodge Lane, Parsippany, NJ 07054
(973) 331-9391

Also available from Eye On Education

**What Great Principals Do *Differently*:
15 Things That Matter Most**
Todd Whitaker

**What Successful Principals Do!
169 Tips for Principals**
Franzy Fleck

BRAVO Principal!
Sandra Harris

**The Administrator's Guide to
School Community Relations, Second Edition**
George E. Pawlas

**Stepping Outside Your Comfort Zone:
Lessons for School Leaders**
Nelson Beaudoin

Dealing with Difficult Teachers, Second Edition
Todd Whitaker

**Dealing with Difficult Parents
(And with Parents in Difficult Situations)**
Todd Whitaker and Douglas Fiore

Great Quotes for Great Educators
Todd Whitaker and Dale Lumpa

**What Great Teachers Do *Differently*:
14 Things That Matter Most**
Todd Whitaker

**Motivating & Inspiring Teachers
The Educational Leader's Guide for Building Staff Morale**
Todd Whitaker, Beth Whitaker, and Dale Lumpa

**The Principal as Instructional Leader:
A Handbook for Supervisors**
Sally J. Zepeda

Six Types of Teachers: Recruiting, Retaining, and Mentoring the Best
Douglas J. Fiore and Todd Whitaker

Instructional Leadership for School Improvement
Sally J. Zepeda

Supervision Across the Content Areas
Sally J. Zepeda and R. Stewart Mayers

**The ISLLC Standards in Action:
A Principal's Handbook**
Carol Engler

**Harnessing the Power of Resistance:
A Guide for Educators**
Jared Scherz

**Achievement Now!
How To Assure No Child is Left Behind**
Dr. Donald J. Fielder

**101 Answers for New Teachers and Their Mentors:
Effective Teaching Tips for Daily Classroom Use**
Annette L. Breaux

Data Analysis for Continuous School Improvement
Victoria L. Bernhardt

**School Leader Internship: Developing, Monitoring,
and Evaluating Your Leadership Experience**
Gary Martin, William Wright, and Arnold Danzig

**Handbook on Teacher Evaluation:
Assessing and Improving Performance**
James Stronge & Pamela Tucker

**Handbook on Teacher Portfolios
for Evaluation and Professional Development**
Pamela Tucker & James Stronge

Dedication

To all my colleagues, students,
and their families,
whose insights and support
led me in my work
as teacher and principal.

Meet the Author

Jane Clark Lindle carries on the family business of education. She is a third generation teacher following in the footsteps of her two grandmothers and a grandfather. Her father is a retired Physics professor from the University of North Carolina-Greensboro. Her mother is a retired kindergarten teacher. Lindle began her career teaching in after-school programs for students with poor literacy and in summer programs for students with behavior problems, including some who had juvenile criminal records. As a special education teacher, Lindle served public and private schools in identifying and designing services for students with disabilities. She's taught students from ages 4 years through 78 years in five states: Kentucky, North Carolina, Pennsylvania, South Carolina, and Wisconsin. She's taught all subject matter in public and parochial schools. She's been principal in three elementary and middle schools across two states. Lindle's academic work focuses on accountability influences on school leadership and shared decision making. She's the immediate past Editor of *Educational Administration Quarterly*, the oldest scholarly journal in the field. Currently, Lindle is Eugene T. Moore Distinguished Professor of Educational Leadership at Clemson University.

Table of Contents

Introduction 1
   What Is Collaborative Leadership? 1
   Sources of the 20 Strategies 2
   Principals and Collaborative Leadership 4
   Organization of the Book 6

Chapter 1—Why Schools Need Collaborative Leaders .. 9
   1. Collaborative School Leaders Know What
      They Stand For 13
         Example of a Political Dance 15
   2. Collaborative School Leaders Find Out What
      Other People Stand For 20
   3. Collaborative School Leaders Seek Conflict,
      Find Problems, and Make Connections 22
   4. Collaborative School Leaders Think Creatively,
      Stimulate Humor, and Inspire Generosity 27
         Humor and Meeting Attendance 28
         Humor in Change 29
   5. Collaborative School Leaders Teach Hope 31
      Summary 33

Chapter 2—Student Achievement and Discipline 37
         I Got Rights 39
   6. Collaborative School Leaders Share Instructional
      Opportunities, Choices, and Wisdom 43
   7. Collaborative School Leaders Dispel Myths and
      Counter Gossip 49
   8. Collaborative School Leaders Use Data and
      Language to Share Experiences 51
   9. Collaborative School Leaders are Principally
      Principled Teachers for Everyone 53
   10. Collaborative School Leaders Ensure Positive
       Teacher–Student Relationships 54
         Figure 2.1. Beginning of the Year Blank Grade Book .. 56
         Figure 2.2. Hypothetical Class with US Census
            Demographics 60

11. Collaborative School Leaders Leverage
    Community Support for Students,
    Teachers, and Their Families 62
        Figure 2.3—Hypothetical Staff with US Census
            Demographics 64
        Summary 66

Chapter 3—School Culture and Community 69
12. Collaborative School Leaders Monitor
    the Environment 71
        Nice Day to Go to the Track 72
13. Collaborative School Leaders Maintain
    the Health of the Environment 78
14. Collaborative School Leaders Honor
    a Student-Centered Culture over
    an Adult-Centered Culture 79
        Math in the Morning 80
        Summary 86

Chapter 4—Administrivia 89
15. Collaborative School Leaders Delegate and Check 95
16. Collaborative School Leaders Follow the Owner's
    Manual for Regular Maintenance 96
17. Collaborative School Leaders Recognize the Sound
    of a Smoothly Running Engine 98
        Don't Tell Me, I Don't Want to Hear It 99
18. Collaborative School Leaders Set Goals
    and Monitor Indicators 104
        Summary 106

Chapter 5—Attending to the Health and Welfare
            of Collaborative Leaders 109
19. Collaborative School Leaders Maintain
    Their Physical Health 112
20. Collaborative School Leaders Maintain
    Their Mental Health 115
        Summary 119

Introduction

What is Collaborative Leadership?

According to common interpretation, a *collaboration* within the school community is a peaceful and placid state of agreement among all parties. However, authentic collaboration requires recognition and exposure of the conflicts inherent in any school environment. All of the parties must negotiate to reach agreement and collaboration. Collaboration implies cooperation, but among the multiparty interests in schooling, collaboration can also trigger contests between each cooperatively formed alliance.

Two common sources of disagreement arise in every school community. They include (1) the abundance of issues about human nature in schools and (2) the shortage of school resources. Very often, the shortage of resources appears obvious to all. Sometimes school leaders, students, parents, guardians, and community members have difficulty identifying issues associated with human nature, human growth, and development. Sometimes the parties do not want to admit the degree of the problems associated with the human issues they face. Students' needs and aspirations challenge every school, but communities, parents, or guardians also have needs that challenge schools. In addition, teachers and other school staff present their own sets of human needs and wants. From students to community to school personnel, many people cannot express, or do not want to reveal, the depth of their needs. Nevertheless, collaboration is not possible unless the parties uncover their problems. To achieve collaboration, the parties must bring the problems to the surface. Collaborative school leaders understand that every school faces both the problems of every aspect of the human condition as well the problems of unending shortages. Therefore, rather than placid peacemakers, collaborative leaders are instigators of both conflict and cooperation.

Collaborative leaders are proactive problem seekers. They are data monitors and good listeners. Collaborative leaders remain sensitive to the various indicators of school and students' needs. They study school and community data trends in order to shore up necessary school community alliances and ensure adequate resources to address students' requirements.

Collaborative leaders recognize the necessity of building coalitions both within the school and among segments of the school community. They listen for signs of discord among any of the school's constituents.

Although collaborative leaders pay attention to informal signals and systematic trends in the school and the community, they also remain sensitive to their impact on others. They remain self-aware so that they can address the consequences of their position of power. Based on their self-awareness, they find ways to make themselves more accessible to all members of the school community. They open themselves to students, parents, and teachers, as well as to members of the larger public and the media. Collaborative leaders refrain from unilateral action, but they also prepare themselves intellectually and creatively for various options in addressing the emerging and perennial issues of schooling.

Collaborative leadership is not a new concept. The current conditions of schools and their politicized environments demand a more collaborative stance from school leaders. School leaders need to renew their attention to the strategies necessary for collaboration. This book provides a chief set of 20 strategies for school leaders to apply in their practice of collaborative leadership.

Sources of the 20 Strategies

Based on the author's various experiences over 30 years in education, this book offers a set of strategies for school leaders. The author generated these strategies from practical experiences as a special education teacher and school principal across four states and five schools. In addition, through her research and service concerning educational leadership as a professor, the author has observed classrooms and principals in over 120 schools. The schools included elementary, middle schools, high schools, vocational centers, and alternative programs in public and nonpublic education systems. Even though some of these schools functioned more smoothly than others did, and some produced more evidence of benefits to their students and communities than others did, none of the schools was free of conflict or competition among school stakeholders. Nevertheless, even the worst of these schools also harbored collaborations and productive partnerships among its stakeholders. Yet problems arose from a failure to use those partnerships to benefit students.

Based on these experiences and observations, the author's primary contention is that school leaders must make *good education* accessible to all students, and to do that, school leaders must find ways to collaborate with many people and groups. Collaborative school leaders serve students best by assembling community resources, supporting teaching and learning, and inspiring hope for each and every student from all school stakeholders. Consequently, school leaders cannot act independently. Instead, school leaders must lead collaboratively.

The author acknowledges the contentious nature of schools. On a daily basis, school leaders confront problems and commotion. By contrast with the average school leader, a collaborative leader seeks problems and heads for, rather than avoids, commotion. This means that collaboration starts disagreements and reveals problems. In short, collaborative school leaders mix it up.

To guide such a stir-it-up approach to leadership, the author offers 20 strategies for school leaders. Although school administrators in any formal school or district position might profit from this concise list of strategies, these 20 strategies derive from the author's work with elementary and secondary building principals. Nearly all of the examples described for these strategies stem from building-level leadership issues. While many school leaders require collaborative skills for serving their specific programs and groups, the building principal faces the greatest diversity of issues but at the same time possesses wide latitude for addressing, or failing to address, the student body's requirements.

Principals and Collaborative Leadership

Recently, a perceived shortage in principal candidates has occupied the attention of researchers and the media. These groups express a belief that the principal's job is both undesirable and undoable. They make dire pronouncements blaming accountability policies as well as increasingly contentious social issues for the shortage of applicants. Perhaps social conditions in some regions can explain some shortages in the pool of candidates for principal positions. For example, as with most jobs, the aging U.S. population of principals has reached retirement age with fewer workers to replace them. Reports show that enough people hold principal certification although they may not apply for every principal position that opens.

Do viable candidates fail to apply because of the much-touted escalating workload of principals? Some reports fail to support these dire beliefs, while others speculate wildly about the difficulty of the job. Those who worry about increasing expectations for principals' work often forget that good principals share leadership. Studies of effective schools for more than 30 years report the importance of shared leadership in increasing student learning. Among those who hold mistaken ideas about the degree of difficulty for principals' work, they also misread the possibilities inherent in the conflicts associated with schooling. Conflicts can breed collaboration.

Educational leaders, more than any other kind of leader, are positioned to exploit conflict for the creation of collaboration. Other kinds of leaders—business, political or even religious leaders—do not have the same connection to a variety of community interests that schools and school leaders have. Other leaders may have more material resources than school leaders. Of course, religious leaders have a different kind of spiritual, emotional, and human capital than school leaders. However, school leaders have a wealth of social networks that they can employ to address students' needs.

Such social networks include students' extended families and, through those families, links to communities. Social services fit into the connections to families, health services, and churches as well as to other social agencies and organizations. Business networks weave through the families and community in sparse or thick connections, depending on the socioeconomic conditions in the area. In addition, schools have links to other schools or institutions of higher education, and those links also vary in strength from community to community. School principals possess the position and the power to tighten or loosen the bindings among these social networks.

Although principals are in positions of power, power is not enough to weave the social fabric necessary to meet students' needs and solve school and community conflicts. Principals must have the foresight to recognize the diversity of the social networks available to serve the school's needs. They also must remain sensitive to the individuals and groups in the social network. Many social groups in a school community so overshadow others that a casual observer may not notice all of the subgroups and individuals in the community. Sometimes a social network may seem smaller than it is because of the overwhelming influence of a few. School leaders must discern the differentials in power among school community members and groups. Principals are in a unique position to judge the connections within the social network surrounding students, parents, and teachers. Principals must appreciate both the vocal and the marginalized groups or individuals. Given their positions of power, principals may be confronted by the more vocal groups, but also have the vantage point from which to identify the marginalized groups and then reach out to them.

In other words, principals have both power and responsibility. Nevertheless, in most U.S. school communities, power is highly contested, and for most principals, their responsibility as leaders is challenged by two perennial conditions of schooling: (1) a shortage of resources and (2) an abundance of human dynamics. Schools are the social institutions that center social services on growth and development. By its nature, the work of human development comes with a full range of human talents and quirks, and no social institution could possibly obtain enough resources to address every possible human want or need. Schools are notoriously under-resourced, yet, simultaneously, they are located where every possible human want and need can surface. It is the principal who occupies a position, shared by no one else, which exposes school shortages and human needs. The principal's power rests with that vantage point. His or her responsibility is to ensure that the school obtains and offers choices in response to shortages of resources and the abundance of needs.

Reactive principals may choose to bemoan the shortages and try to ignore or stifle the needs. These principals strive to avoid conflicts and dampen the turmoil surrounding schools. In contrast, proactive principals move collaboratively to share their vantage point on needs. They promote conflict to help those with resources to face the needs of those who are without. They work to make connections between groups and individuals who may never have worked together before. They make the uncomfortable more comfortable, but they may disturb those who do not understand or recognize the needs and conflicts around them. Finally, collaborative principals leverage resources to address the needs of schools and students.

While the complexity of school conflict and student needs should never be minimized, school leaders must find a way of calming the chaos and providing certainty when ambiguity reigns. In the face of these requirements for calm and certainty, exposing conflicts and problems may seem counterintuitive, but such strategies reassure school communities and help to keep school stakeholders' focus on students.

Organization of the Book

In the interest of developing more collaborative principals, this book provides 20 strategies. Five chapters explain the purpose of the 20 strategies. In each chapter, a subset of strategies is described along with examples from the author's collection of journal notes, field observations, and case studies. The strategies follow the order in which collaborative school leaders need to approach their work.

Chapter 1 explains strategies 1 through 5, which provide a foundation for the collaborative leader's practice.

> Strategy 1—Collaborative School Leaders Know What They Stand For
>
> Strategy 2—Collaborative School Leaders Find Out What Other People Stand For
>
> Strategy 3—Collaborative School Leaders Seek Conflict, Find Problems, and Make Connections
>
> Strategy 4—Collaborative School Leaders Think Creatively, Stimulate Humor, and Inspire Generosity
>
> Strategy 5—Collaborative School Leaders Teach Hope

Chapter 2 sets students as the focus and highest priority of collaborative leaders' work. This chapter covers strategies 6 though 11, which concern student achievement, discipline, and social service needs.

> Strategy 6—Collaborative School Leaders Share Instructional Opportunities, Choices, and Wisdom
>
> Strategy 7—Collaborative School Leaders Dispel Myths and Counter Gossip
>
> Strategy 8—Collaborative School Leaders Use Data and Language to Share Experiences
>
> Strategy 9—Collaborative School Leaders are Principally Principled Teachers for Everyone
>
> Strategy 10—Collaborative School Leaders Ensure Positive Teacher–Student Relationships
>
> Strategy 11—Collaborative School Leaders Leverage Community Support for Students, Teachers and Their Families

Chapter 3 focuses on the internal culture of the school. Strategies 12 through 14 address the collaborative leader's relationship to and responsibilities concerning teachers and support staff.

Strategy 12—Collaborative School Leaders Monitor the Environment

Strategy 13—Collaborative School Leaders Maintain the Health of the Environment

Strategy 14—Collaborative School Leaders Honor a Student-Centered Culture over an Adult-Centered Culture

In chapter 4, strategies 15 through 18 encompass the routines and systems that a well-run school possesses. Despite the flippancy of the title "Administrivia," chapter 4 deals with the fundamentals common to data interpretation and systems management.

Strategy 15—Collaborative School Leaders Delegate and Check

Strategy 16—Collaborative School Leaders Follow the Owner's Manual for Regular Maintenance

Strategy 17—Collaborative School Leaders Recognize the Sound of a Smoothly Running Engine

Strategy 18—Collaborative School Leaders Set Goals and Monitor Indicators

Finally, chapter 5 offers strategies for coping in the high-stress and sometimes traumatic environment of school leadership. Approaches such as strategies 19 and 20 rarely appear in the manuals or texts for educational leaders.

Strategy 19—Collaborative School Leaders Maintain Their Physical Health

Strategy 20—Collaborative School Leaders Maintain Their Mental Health

Every chapter provides examples of good and bad forms of collaborative leadership. Each example derives from authentic composites of the author's experiences recorded in journals and field notes from her practice and observations of other school leaders. Readers should interact with the text and reflect on the ways in which their leadership practices approach or retreat from a collaborative approach to leadership.

Chapter 1
Why Schools Need Collaborative Leaders

Strategies 1 through 5 for Collaborative School Leaders

1. Collaborative School Leaders Know What They Stand For
2. Collaborative School Leaders Find Out What Other People Stand For
3. Collaborative School Leaders Seek Conflict, Find Problems, and Make Connections
4. Collaborative School Leaders Think Creatively, Stimulate Humor, and Inspire Generosity
5. Collaborative School Leaders Teach Hope

Schools need collaborative leaders because education is as pervasive an activity as breathing, everyone has a stake in schools and students, and almost anyone has an opinion about what a *good education* ought to be and what teachers, parents, and students ought to do. Opinions provide options, but choosing among the options requires knowledge and wisdom, in other words—leadership.

Some of the writing and griping about school administrators reflects badly on individuals who managed rather than led teachers and students to a *good education*. That kind of distinction between management and leadership may be harsh. Previous generations of school administrators fulfilled their communities' expectations for *keeping schools*. Today, communities hold the higher expectation that every student receive the benefits of a good education. These communities want more than a well-kept school; they expect teachers and school leaders to *teach* school. However, what these communities mean by a good education differs not only from one community to the next, but also within a single school's community.

The clamor of demands, wants, and expectations surrounding schools requires leaders who can sort through the abundance of opinions, solutions, and options. Schools and students need leaders who focus every conversation on how that conversation increases good education for every student. Schools need leaders who can negotiate progress rather than mediate a paralyzing truce. Paralyzing truces result from so-called leaders who take the safer path for themselves, who avoid risks and conflicts without regard to the potential results for students. Paralysis prevents school improvement and student achievement.

Children grow up so fast that many adults cannot adjust to their changes. School leaders have to overcome the inertia of an adult-intensive enterprise to respond to students' needs. School leaders must infuse urgency at the same time that they preside over all of the human and humane elements of schools such as rituals, routines, ceremonies, and stages of growth and development. School leaders head a constant search for balance among the competing needs and interests of students, families, and communities. The source of that elusive equilibrium resides among those applying the pressure, and school leaders must enlist the active participation of every stakeholder in achieving the ends of a *good education*.

Schools need collaborative school leaders because schools harbor conflict and contests in every moment and act of teaching and learning. Unlike stakeholders, school leaders hold a unique overview of the variety and glut of conflicts and contests. School leaders can explain, demonstrate, inspire, mediate, and leverage from a vantage point unlike any other in schools or any other enterprise.

On the other hand, if school leaders act unilaterally, then competition and conflicts become more intense and petrified. Authoritative leaders fossilize schools. Schools lose the fluidity necessary to meet ever-changing student needs when the school leader alienates or marginalizes any member of the school community. Schools represent a significant hub in the web of social networks for the larger community, and school leaders who ignore the interconnectedness of schools and communities sever ties that bind. Independent, authoritative action polarizes and estranges.

Schools need collaborative school leaders because no school ever has enough resources to address all of the needs of every student. A school's only and greatest wealth is the student body. Students provide the primary source of human capital that schools use to obtain other material resources. Schools need leaders who can tighten the social links among the student body to the larger community. Using these links, school leaders must beg, leverage, borrow, and arouse others to provide the means necessary for a *good education*.

School leaders can use five strategies for establishing collaborative leadership in a way that legitimately addresses a *good education* for each and every student. The five strategies in this chapter supply a foundation for the practice of collaborative leadership in the remaining 15 strategies. The foundation rests on the collaborative leader's self-awareness. From a stance of self-awareness, a collaborative school leader can encourage the entire school community to offer every student opportunities and choices, and the wisdom to deal with both.

Strategy 1
Collaborative School Leaders Know What They Stand For

Collaborative school leaders remain clear about the primary goal of their work. They sustain that clarity by consistently focusing on the people for whom they work—the students. They have a laser-straight and laser-intense sense of purpose in providing a good education to every student.

Schools roil with competing interests and contradictory aims. Collaboration requires clear statements about all of the opportunities and choices represented by the school stakeholders in their competition to achieve their particular goals. School leaders achieve clarity by stating their principles openly and confidently.

Collaborative school leaders operate from the premise that every act associated with schooling must lead to better opportunities and accomplishments for each student. That premise means that every conversation, each moment, and every activity leads to benefits for every pupil. The school leader asks one consistent, principled, and clarifying question of everyone involved in schools: How does this benefit students? The question can be formed in various ways, but it applies to any situation:

- How does this curricular program benefit students?
- How does this extra- or co-curricular activity benefit students?
- How does this discussion benefit students?
- How does this purchase benefit students?
- How does this school dance benefit students?
- How does this parent's complaint expose something that benefits or harms students?

Because school environments are chaotic and filled with distractions, collaborative school leaders can relieve that profuse confusion by keeping the central focus on students. Many accounts and research studies note the logistical pressures of too many students and too little time to serve their needs adequately. Daily life in schools reels from time compression and scarce resources. As a result, most messages, memos, conversations, and meetings float on the minutia of how to get things done. By attending to the trivial steps of getting things done, school personnel lose their perspective on the purposes of schooling. When school leaders reshape all conversations to the singular question, "How does this benefit students?" the school's primary purpose re-emerges. Collaborative principals reshape the conflicts about schools by placing students at the center of attention.

Schools have served multiple agendas, but their *core purpose* is student achievement. Collaborative school leaders realize the core of their work is students' learning: teaching school. Repeated reports state that many teachers obtain certification for the principalship for reasons other than serving students.[1] Collaborative principals hold their work with students as a sacred trust. They believe that providing every student a good education drives their work with students, parents, guardians, teachers, staff, and the community.

People in positions of power, principals included, suffer a variety of projections about their motives for attaining such a position. People may assume that the principal's ambitions included a desire to give orders, get a large paycheck, or fulfill a hunger for power over students, teachers, parents, and other community members. Collaborative leaders blunt the speculations by openly discussing their reasons for taking on a leadership role. They explain their motives and ambitions. They recognize that unanswered speculations engender damaging suppositions and distracting gossip. To thwart gossip, collaborative leaders provide straightforward answers about themselves and their ambitions.

When school leaders expose their motives openly, they inspire others to reveal their positions. School leaders who refrain from revealing their positions may believe that they have left

---

[1] Some reports show that people seek the raises that accompany added graduate courses or certification even if they do not use the certificate by serving as a principal.

room for other people to share their dreams, but usually a reticent school leader impedes opportunities for others. People open up their agenda when a school leader is open. When a school leader models an appropriate manner to express an educational goal, the reaction from others can be one of two responses: (1) an equally clear and open contradiction to the leader's position or (2) an agreement with the leader's stated agenda. Either response is more desirable than the confusing dance of political machinations generated from each stakeholder's guarded probes about meaning and purposes.

The following example demonstrates the debilitating effects of a leader's lack of candor. It represents a familiar sampling of the kinds of interactions that drive people to headaches and avoidance of meetings.

Example of a Political Dance

A school faculty meeting started at its regularly scheduled time on Tuesday afternoon after the dismissal of students. The principal and twenty-three teachers assembled in the school library. Canned soft drinks and a plate of cookies sat on a table next to a sign-in sheet. The school librarian trolled the tables making sure that everyone was using a paper napkin for a coaster on the wooden tables. The following exchange occurred in the initial 20 minutes of the faculty meeting.

Principal: The district office says we need to write a mission statement for our school.

Teacher 1: What's wrong with the one we have?

Principal: It's too long.

Teacher 2: We have a mission statement?

Principal: We wrote it about two years before you came.

Teacher 1: That took forever. I don't want to go through that again.

Teacher 3: I thought the discussions were very eye opening.

Teacher 4: I was here two years ago and I don't remember anything about this.

> *Teacher 5:* Think it through. That was two years before she came, not two years ago.
>
> *Teacher 4:* Oh, well, I've been here longer, and I don't remember anything about a mission statement.
>
> *Principal:* Well, we need to write something now. Does anyone want to start? What do we believe about the mission of our school?
>
> *Teacher 5:* Give me your tired, your cranky, your disrespectful, and your wanna-be rock stars and jocks yearning for discovery.

Most of the faculty laughs. The principal's head nods as his face forms a bemused expression.

> *Teacher 2:* I wish I knew what the current mission statement says.
>
> *Teacher 6:* It's on the school calendar. I was on the committee that said it should be there.
>
> *Teacher 2:* Does anyone have a school calendar?
>
> *Principal:* We can get one for everyone.
>
> *Teacher 1:* Well, when? I don't think we should start writing anything new until we've all had a chance to look at the old mission statement and start from there.

Other teachers nod their heads or call out "yes."

> *Principal:* You know, like everything else, this is due yesterday. We need to start now.
>
> *Teacher 5:* What do you think we're supposed to say if our old one is too long?
>
> *Principal:* What I think isn't that important. This is supposed to represent what the school community thinks.
>
> *Teacher 1:* I think we need to look over the original mission statement before we open this can of worms.
>
> *Teacher 4:* Sounds like we should have some parents write this too.
>
> *Teacher 3:* Yeah, and students should have some say in it.

Principal: Could we start with some criteria that we believe so that we can figure out if the old mission statement fits and for these other groups to have something to use to evaluate it?

Teacher 2: Can you give me an example of what you mean by *criteria*?

Principal: If I give you an example, then I'm afraid that it might color your answers. Just finish this sentence, 'We believe . . .'

Teacher 5 [singing]: We believe with every drop of paint that falls, asbestos grows . . .

Several teachers laugh. Then the room settles to an awkward silence. The principal sighs audibly with tightened lips.

Teacher 1: Maybe you could send the original mission statement to everyone, and then underneath it we all could write two or three endings to the 'We believe . . .' beginning.

Many teachers nod, and a few "yeses" are voiced.

Principal: Well, ok, but I think we'll need an extra faculty meeting or two to meet the district's deadline with that kind of circulation.

The room erupts in groans.

Teacher 5: Does the district have something we could read so we know what they want?

Principal: Not really. It's just something that came up at the principals' meeting.

The above example illustrates the kind of paralysis that poor leaders generate when they are coy about their motives. The implicit message in this vignette is that the principal just needs to fulfill a task set by the district. The content and veracity of the school's mission statement seems an ancillary point. More than the principal, the teachers keep trying to deal with the content of the mission statement. Yet the teachers also participate in delaying any direct evaluation of the current mission statement or initiation of a new mission statement. Within these 20 minutes of posturing and stalling, what would be the answer to the seminal question: How does this meeting benefit students?

After almost 20 minutes, the meeting has stalled, the cookies have been eaten, the canned drinks have been consumed, and despite the feeding frenzy, everyone is frustrated. Given this scene, the likely outcome is that the principal will not fulfill the district's directive however wise or ill advised that edict might be. Indeed, the principal suggests a hidden motive by not being forthcoming about what the district's purpose might be, and the teachers must question the principal repeatedly in order to gain any information about the expectations for the task. Teachers also resist proceeding. The result is an ugly waste of time, which is a scarce resource for schools—one that schools cannot afford to abuse.

A collaborative school leader could have elicited more from the faculty with two simple steps. Both steps encompass the strategy of clarifying what the leader stands for. First, the collaborative leader could have prepared for the meeting. The preparation could have included giving each teacher a copy of the current school mission statement and any other relevant materials from the district's meeting with the principals. Second, the collaborative leader could have prepared an opening statement that covered the following:

1. When and why the district wanted new or revised school mission statements

2. A brief synopsis of when, how, and why the school's previous mission statement had been constructed

3. A short list of school issues and conditions that are similar or different from those stated in the original mission statement

4. A set of choices among steps that the faculty could follow in revising the old or developing a new mission statement

5. Insertion of commentary wherever necessary that signaled when the collaborative leader was expressing an opinion or belief of his/her own as opposed to relaying a district command or policy.

Although human nature is such that even with such preparation, faculty members might ask clarifying questions, the chances are greater that this preparation would stimulate a substantive discussion. The faculty's work could have proceeded about the advantages and disadvantages of the school's current mission statement. In any case, a leader's revelation of his or her stance regarding the mission statement assignment potentially would lead the group closer to fulfilling the task than the above dance produced.

Even though many people resist orders, they are less frustrated at complying with demands that are clear, concise, and openly acknowledge the conditions of the requirement than when the directions appear covert and uncertain. Moreover, in an open exchange, people are more likely to be frank about their beliefs. Groups that are engaged in probing the leader's beliefs waste precious school time. A leader's failure to speak plainly leads to others' guardedness. Collaborative leaders need to know what others believe and think in order to make opportunities better for students. They start by modeling the kind of openness about personal visions, goals, and ambitions that they need from others.

Strategy 2
Collaborative School Leaders Find Out What Other People Stand For

With a range of stakeholders from the students to school personnel to families and businesses, school leaders face both imaginable and unimaginable expectations. Collaborative school leaders need to understand the various expectations they face. They also need to recognize that they cannot please everyone.

School leaders with a collaborative stance understand others' purposes. Such school leaders accept that other people's expectations differ for a number of reasons. School leaders who have teaching experience use their background with the diversity of students' needs, wants, and paces of development. Those school leaders apply their background with student diversity to their colleagues, students, parents, and other adults with a stake in education.

In other words, elementary and secondary schools cannot limit human development to within classroom walls. Every adult is a learner with needs. Thus, learning happens in faculty rooms as well as in any place the adults gather. Adults have as many differences in their learning skills and knowledge as children, but adults' lives are more complicated. Adults have added responsibilities distracting them from understanding new challenges or adapting to different requirements. Unlike most children, many adults think they have nothing left to learn, just because they have so many responsibilities as well as rights. Therefore, while students present an array of learning challenges, adults present just as many plus a lot more along with more complications.

Just as teachers have to use a wide ranges of strategies to identify students' needs, school leaders must use all of those strategies to better understand the needs of students and adults. Along with those needs, adults may also express their desires and expectations, or they may not express anything at all. School leaders need to unearth the wide variety of people's desires and expectations concerning schools. Collaborative school leaders make allowances for the developmental needs of students as well as the concerns of the adults associated with those students. Beyond the developmental learning needs of students and of the adults associated with them, these leaders seek to understand other people's agendas.

Collaborative school leaders recognize that collaboration is not a process of resolving, smoothing over, or avoiding conflict. On the contrary, collaboration is a process of seeking, uncovering, and naming problems so that the inevitable conflict associated with schooling is exposed and addressed.

Strategy 3
Collaborative School Leaders Seek Conflict, Find Problems, and Make Connections

The dynamics of school communities produces innumerable sources of conflict for schools. For the purposes of promoting collaborative school leaders who manage that conflict successfully, this strategy focuses on four such sources as follows:

1. Schooling in a diverse society can mean everyone is right and everyone is wrong, simultaneously.
2. Human foibles are the raw material of both leadership and education.
3. Common sense is neither simple nor common.
4. Schools never have enough of anything, except people. (See conflict 2 above.)

Understanding these four sources of conflict in schools helps school leaders to recognize problems and to proactively intervene in the process of solving them before they escalate or cause harm to students. Every one of these sources stems from a set of circumstances that characterize all schools.

The first source of conflict derives from community diversity. Although some educators lament diversity because its management requires creativity and insight, no school anywhere on earth is wholly homogeneous. Because each person is different, any classroom, anywhere in the world, holds an array of student talents and needs. Hence, every school, which by definition holds more than one classroom, multiplies the array and variety of student abilities and disabilities. Schools, classrooms, and students require different remedies for their needs. Any given solution could be right for one pupil, but highly inappropriate for another. The discord that can arise between proponents of one educational practice and another can be passionate and all together both right and wrong. The probability is high that facing differences creates disputes.

The second source of conflict is related to the diversity of students. Many school conflicts arise from the raw material of both education and leadership, that is, human beings. Schooling includes all stages of human development from early childhood through adulthood. Everyone involved in schools represents his or her own set of personal gifts and shortcomings. What's more, unlike any other social institution, the school community combines children and adults. A school's unique mix of pupils and teachers as well as other involved adults means that a lifespan of developmental issues foments conflict throughout the school community.

For example, children may be dealing with issues of dependence and independence at the same moment that a teacher or parent is wrestling with the same issues, but with different behaviors and different levels of self-awareness. As noted with the first source of conflict, differences breed competition for attention and resources. The competitors vie for resolution by offering low-cost solutions, and sometimes the minimal cost represents something other than money. Complexity wears people out; thus, a simple solution may seduce them. In fact, oversimplicity ironically seduces school communities into more conflict.

The third source of conflict in schools often springs from the rhetoric of common sense. Turbulent communities often use words as cheap weapons. In the intense environment of schools, people want straightforwardness. But overly simple answers to complex problems make more problems and uncover other unrecognized conflicts. Collaborative school leaders do not overreact by seeking elaborate and confusing resolutions, but they do help their school communities understand complexity. Such leaders promote collaboration among students, teachers, parents, and community groups that extends their understanding of complexity. At the heart of these explanations, collaborative school leaders seek resolutions. For each option among the resolutions, these leaders return to the central question: How does this benefit students? Collaborative school leaders counteract seductive, overly simplistic rhetoric by refocusing the search for solutions on addressing the diversity and variety of student needs. All of those different needs require complex solutions because they require many resources.

Competition for resources spotlights the fourth source of conflict for schools. Schools cannot supply all of the resources necessary for everyone. Schools are always short of money, materials, time, energy, or cooperation. As a result, everyone in a school has to be an entrepreneur. Teachers recycle and beg. Leaders beg and hunt for new donors, and they invent. However, if school personnel and/or their communities are not inventive, they turn to fighting over the scraps. The collaborative leader must stimulate creativity and seek new ways of fulfilling school needs.

By understanding the sources of school conflict, collaborative leaders remain alert to signs that any of these sources might disturb the equilibrium of their school community. Collaborative school leaders develop ways to map the connections among all of the people in the community. They monitor the hub of the social networks, the school, and they follow the connections from the school to the community. They pay attention to groups that are thinly connected to and marginalized by the school and the school community. They also keep in perspective the vocal and influential groups associated with students and their families. Collaborative leaders understand that sensitivity to emerging disruptions in these networks may also lead to the connections necessary for settling the disturbance.

But recognizing disturbances does not automatically settle them. Even though a collaborative approach may appear to be a means of calming the conflicts that plague schools, uncovering those conflicts may increase the clamor. Some people benefit more than others do from suppressing conflict. Those people may be very angry with a leader who reveals problems and points out ways that people are not acting collaboratively. Sometimes, collaborative leaders have to live with bearing the brunt of conflicts that come from uncovering a hidden problem. Thus, not only do schools bear four constant sources of conflict; school leaders risk creating further conflicts through addressing any of those four problems, but they do so to effect necessary changes. The following is a simple example of how a school leader can uncover problems and stimulate conflict, yet do so for the benefit of students.

As schools struggle with safety issues, one of the first steps is to look at the number and types of student disruptions that might pose a threat to school safety. A principal, assistant principal, or guidance counselor may analyze school records in order to determine such data as the following: (1) how many students were involved in fights, (2) when and where the fights occurred, and (3) which teachers were involved in stopping the fights or sending the students to the office for consequences.

While the first two sets of records, student numbers and time and place of fights, seem directly related to school safety issues, the last set may be vaguer and may be very controversial. The last data set, which involves teachers, may reveal some important information related to school safety. On the one hand, this information about teachers may show that only a few teachers are willing or able to stop fights. Nevertheless, that fact raises a question: While their actions lower the chance of injury from the violence, what are the other teachers doing to diffuse the potential for future violence? On the other hand, this teacher information could lead to further investigation of why certain teachers send more students to the office for fighting. Are these teachers less aware of what is going on with students until the problem spins out of control? While responsible adults who remain alert to the ways students act are the best means of increasing school safety, some teachers may feel that the job of teaching should not include prevention of student violence. When collaborative school leaders collect and report data about teachers' actions related to student fights, they may expose teachers who avoid preventing or intervening in student fights. Those teachers may become angry with the leaders who investigate their actions or lack of action. However, despite any anger among the faculty, school leaders must make the school safer for students as well as teachers. Part of making schools safe includes making sure that the adults, including teachers, take the right actions to reduce student violence.

Schools exist in neighborhoods. What happens in the neighborhoods filters into the schools. In many schools, basic steps in the creation of a safer school environment include getting support from the neighbors, from the individuals who own houses or businesses in the area. Schools need their neighbors' support as well as the attention of local law enforcement. School principals can make those connections with neighbors, businesses, and the police as well as with such important figures as judges.

Collaborative leaders live with conflict and choose to stimulate it, mediate it, or alleviate it based on what is beneficial to students. They reach out to find out what is working and what is not. They reach out to identify connections and disruptions, and they make connections for the purpose of improving students' opportunities and experiences. By finding problems and forging alliances, collaborative leaders bring to bear the abundance of human capital that schools require to address their paucity of material resources.

Strategy 4

Collaborative School Leaders Think Creatively, Stimulate Humor, and Inspire Generosity

Solutions often start with humor. Just as scarcity is the mother of invention, humor drives creativity. Humor cements relationships and opens up imagination.

Collaborative leaders understand that bolstering alliances includes developing trust. Schools need alliances because they cannot provide good education without outside support. Trust ensures that resources will be shared willingly. Humor often speaks to issues of trust.

Deprecating humor divides and reduces trust. For that reason, collaborative leaders never tell demeaning stories about people. The collaborative school leader will never use the term *humor* in reference to any kind of degradation of others. Such leaders avoid telling or tolerating formalized jokes or silly references about specific groups of people or certain characteristics of groups or individuals.

Instead, collaborative leaders may turn to observations that note the idiosyncrasies of shared experiences. They never pretend to share experiences that they have never had. On the contrary, they find a common ground for celebrating similarities or honoring differences. This kind of humor lifts spirits and seals a connection among the parties. The kind of humor that collaborative leaders use encourages all to view their common challenges in a different way.

Collaborative leaders forge alliances with humor for a purpose. That is, when people can view a problem from a different angle, a funny one, they can be more creative in finding solutions. Given the never-ending scarcities in schools, all educational issues require creativity. While schools face the same kinds of human challenges repeatedly, each student's challenge is unique and requires flexibility in dealing with that challenge. By encouraging an open atmosphere for thinking differently, the collaborative leader can stimulate cooperation and solicit assistance to the benefit of all students.

To illustrate the importance of humor in school leadership, the following two examples depict shared experiences that can be viewed innovatively. One of the continual shared experiences of school personnel is attending meetings, and the other is addressing change.

Humor and Meeting Attendance

The middle school principal drops the agenda for the Team Leader Meeting and its handouts on the conference room table as the twelve team leaders file into the room toting their school bags and notepads. They greet each other with polite chitchat. Then one of the younger team leaders sails into the room moaning and complaining.

Younger Team Leader: Meetings, meetings, meetings. I can't believe how much time meetings take, and then afterward there's so much to do. Maybe if we didn't meet we'd not have so much to do. Couldn't we get someone else to go to meetings for us?

Veteran Team Leader [chuckling]: When I first started teaching, all the teachers said the same thing, and then they created this position called *Team Leader* to have someone else go to all the meetings for them.

Principal: Guess what. When I first started teaching, all the teachers said they didn't want to go to any more meetings, so they created this position called *Principal* to have someone else go to all the meetings for them. Where will it all end?

The room erupts in laughter.

Although the humor in this example is not a joke *per se*, it provokes laughter because the principal has chosen to join in the conversation as participant rather than to remain a silent eavesdropper. The principal validates the frustration that many share in the relentless problem of limited time and endless meetings. The laughter stems from realization that the principal shared the veteran teacher's understanding that meetings represent an unavoidable condition of work in schools. Instead of arguing the point, the principal chooses a more light-hearted way to acknowledge the shared frustration.

Besides meetings, change is a constant condition of schooling. Change disturbs routines and requires enormous flexibility for its accommodation. Nevertheless, change is a condition of growth and development and thus is essential to learning. Accordingly, change is a school resource and often seems to be the only abundant resource in schools. Frequently, change is too overwhelming for school personnel to address because of limited resources and the inevitable inertia of people locked in routines. The following scenario shows one school leader's use of humor to gain some momentum in effecting change.

Humor in Change

The budget officer for the school district walks the school board members through the budget draft, explaining the state's constraints on spending as he outlines projected revenues and expenditures. The presentation bogs down because of the school board members' repeated questions about new state regulations on spending for personnel, the board's biggest budget expense. The budget officer patiently tries to answer the questions and parry the board members' rising frustration.

> *Budget Officer:* I feel your pain. Seems like for every step forward I make, I take two steps back in the dance with the state's rules and regulations.
>
> *Superintendent:* Well, that's because you're not leading, but following. Think Fred Astaire, not Ginger Rogers.
>
> *Board Member:* And take off those high heels.

The laughter generated from this exchange placed the ensuing conversation on a different level. Instead of asking questions about the new rules, the board members launched into questions about how to deal with the new rules.

The humor here was at the expense of the budget officer, who took the remarks good naturedly for two reasons: (1) the relationship between the budget officer and the superintendent was strong enough that each trusted the other enough to openly acknowledge his individual talents and limitations, and (2) the exchange pushed the ensuing discussion in the direction that the budget officer had planned for the board presentation. One of the features of leadership in change is that the leader learns of the change before others do and often has moved past the initial shock and grief related to that change before the rest learn of it. In such situations, leaders must be prepared to allow others to express their shock and grief over a change before proceeding to planning ways to deal with the change. The budget officer's comment was an appropriate leaderly observation allowing board members to express their concerns legitimately.

When the board member extended the superintendent's humorous comparison, that quip helped the other members to acknowledge that change presents difficulties. Then they could move past the emotional issues of change and begin to solve the problems. The superintendent's comment stimulated the board member's ability to think differently about the changes, and, thus, the other board members made the shift from lamenting and admiring problems to coping with change. In short, the exchange lifted the shadows that had appeared on their expected path to reveal another path. Laughter raised spirits as well as possibilities.

Strategy 5
Collaborative School Leaders Teach Hope

The public and private benefits of schooling are that both society and individuals experience more opportunities and choices. A *good education* offers its recipients the wisdom to deal with opportunities and choices as a core outcome of schooling. Without wisdom, opportunities and choices may be disturbing and disruptive because consequences are neither certain nor predictable. With an increase in uncertainty often comes pessimism and despair. The promise of education is that individuals and society create a hopeful future.

School leaders hold an important responsibility in schooling to ensure that under their watch, education continues to offer hope and promise to every student. Each student enters school with a variety of potential outcomes, and no one can make a definite prognosis about any of these.

School leaders need to provoke conversations among teachers, parents, and the students themselves that seek the most hopeful opportunities for student development and learning. Sometimes when parents bring outrageously optimistic or pessimistic expectations into their conversations, the school leader has to help them shape their expectations realistically. Realism does not equate with dampening hope, but instead offers opportunities and alternatives. Sometimes teachers become cynical about some students' potential, which school leaders must counteract. School leaders must create the means for ensuring hope among school personnel to benefit every student.

To pursue hope, school leaders must be inventive and optimistic themselves. Much in the environment of schools, however, operates to degrade hope. Schools shelter all of the possible combinations of human talents and faults, expectations and failures. Along with limited time and money, schools are often ill equipped for dealing with the pluses and minuses of human activity. All of the needs for students as well as for professional development seem enormous by comparison with available school resources. Nevertheless, more than any other social institution, schools harbor the single resource of offering hope to society through the education of students.

School leaders must express unshakable belief in the power of education to improve students' potential and create a better future for society. The foundation of that belief must be a certainty and positivism that any problem in social dynamics and every limitation resulting from scarce resources can be surmounted by the inventiveness and energy of school personnel and their communities. School leaders cement hopefulness by nourishing the links and networks among students and families, school personnel and communities. School leaders use collaboration as the means to promote hopeful ends for students.

Collaborative school leaders offer hope and are hopeful because schooling benefits both students and society. The promise of schooling is a better future for all, and collaborative school leaders are the guardians of hope.

Summary

Good education requires a lot of interaction between and among adults and children in schools and in the community. Just as teachers need to master the group dynamics in their classrooms and in interactions with each other, school leaders need to support those efforts at making groups work in classrooms, throughout the school, and among the stakeholders for the school (students, parents, teachers, and community members). School leaders need basic self-awareness and insight into others' interests and motivations in order to orchestrate the harmonies created by the human dynamics in classrooms, schools, neighborhoods and communities to the benefit of students.

This chapter has addressed five strategies for school leaders, which are summarized below, that form the basic platform for a collaborative approach to leadership.

Strategy 1—Collaborative School Leaders Know What They Stand For

- They understand that their work serves others, especially students.
- They understand the difference between *keeping school* and *teaching school*.
- They stay focused on how their work and the contributions of teachers, parents, and community benefit students.
- They make their own attitudes and positions plainly known to all.
- They place an intense and urgent focus on student learning.

Strategy 2—Collaborative School Leaders Find Out What Other People Stand For

- They face the range of expectations held for students and their schools.
- They appreciate diversity and all the conflict that can arise from differing points of view and expectations.
- They understand that the school's stakeholders are adult learners who have developmental issues and needs.
- They expose differing opinions and conflicts so that the school community can work toward resolutions.

Strategy 3—Collaborative School Leaders Seek Conflict, Find Problems, and Make Connections

- They understand that school conflict stems from two main sources: (1) a surplus of people issues ranging from growth to group dynamics and (2) scarce resources in terms of money and time.
- They celebrate diversity because it presents opportunities for creativity and new insights into making schooling better for students.
- They constantly monitor their internal and external environments for signs that schooling is not working adequately for any single student or any group of students.
- They live with conflict, but they do not avoid it or cover it up.
- They lead the school community to creative answers rather than overly simple or expedient ones.

Strategy 4—Collaborative School Leaders Think Creatively, Stimulate Humor, and Inspire Generosity

- They understand that creativity and humor are closely linked.
- They understand that appropriate humor can build group trust and identity.
- They never use humor that degrades anyone or any group.
- They appreciate the humor of predicaments and situations and use it to help people think more imaginatively about solutions.
- They inspire people to be generous in their approach to solutions.

Strategy 5—Collaborative School Leaders Teach Hope

- They understand that education means hope for the future for students, their families, and communities.
- They help students and families find reasonable alternatives to unreasonable aspirations and expectations.
- They help teachers to remain creative and hopeful about their ability to teach *any* and *all* students.
- They find people, organizations, and agencies in the community that support optimistic outcomes from schooling all students and their communities.

Chapter 2

Student Achievement and Discipline

Strategies 6 through 11 for Collaborative School Leaders

6. Collaborative School Leaders Share Instructional Opportunities, Choices, and Wisdom

7. Collaborative School Leaders Dispel Myths and Counter Gossip

8. Collaborative School Leaders Use Data and Language to Share Experiences

9. Collaborative School Leaders are Principally Principled Teachers for Everyone

10. Collaborative School Leaders Ensure Positive Teacher–Student Relationships

11. Collaborative School Leaders Leverage Community Support for Students, Teachers, and Their Families

Student achievement and discipline are the hallmarks of collaborative school leadership. Collaborative school leaders make their marks as instructional leaders by focusing on student achievement and discipline. Student achievement and discipline are entwined with student growth and learning.

Although learning and growth are inevitable, undirected learning and growth are as uncontrollable as breathing and nearly as reflexive. The difference between undirected learning and education is found in the opportunities that emerge from education. Undirected learning often has unintended results and consequences. In contrast, education offers a clear focus and a purpose for learning, and it ensures that results are more predictable. Education encompasses both academic achievement and development of social skills.

Education helps people grow in greater ways than they would have if left to develop without any guidance. While learning is part of growing and training is controlled learning, education not only controls learning, but also prepares people for the future. A *good education* expands benefits beyond growth and training through the development of wisdom. Education offers wisdom as the core benefit for individuals and their communities as a return on their schooling investments.

Schooling occupies a significant amount of students' lives, and every moment in schools ought to be a learning opportunity. Good instruction makes the most of every moment by focusing learning on opportunity, choice, and wisdom. The ultimate goal of education is to prepare students to make the most of their opportunities and choices. Individuals' and society's hopes rest on these benefits of education.

Schools tackle the difficult task of providing opportunities, choices, wisdom, and hope for every student. Every student presents a mix of acceptance of and resistance to instruction. Take the example of Candrero below.

I Got Rights!

Candrero Martines never raised his hand to say anything in class. He had never raised his hand in first grade, and now that he was in sixth grade, he did not plan to start. He simply talked whenever he desired. Often he felt compelled to disagree with the things his teacher said that his mother, big brother, or cousins had told him were not true.

The teacher would say, "If you wait for your turn, you'll get some." But the men in Candrero's family had told him never to wait for anyone or he would lose his turn. Candrero's mother always gave him his portion first at dinner. He received a treat whenever he came in the door from school. Except at school, Candrero never waited for anything. Most of the time at school, he simply cut into a line or fought his way to be first. As a result, all through school, he lost his recess privileges or spent time in the in-school suspension room for this behavior. Over time, he did not change at all.

In sixth grade, his teacher was a little different. She always called on Candrero at the very beginning of class. She even met him at the door and gave him something like a paper or a pencil, just as his mom met him at the door with a pleasant surprise when he came home from school. Nevertheless, Candrero did not raise his hand any more than he used to. But he also did not call out as much as he had before, and he seemed to feel less need to argue with his teacher, until today.

Today was different because of a substitute teacher. The substitute had rules written on the board and started giving demerits to students who did not follow the rules immediately. The demerits, which amounted to pushups or jumping jacks, were assigned the minute the students walked into the room. As always, the students came in talking, but the first rule on the board was, "Don't talk." To prove that she meant business, the substitute had the first six students who chattered as they walked in the door drop to the floor and do pushups. Candrero was one of those students. He was so shocked that without a word, he dropped down and did five pushups with the other students. But that was the end of that. He rose after the fifth pushup and shouted an obscenity as he informed the substitute that he would not do one more pushup.

It was Candrero's bad timing that the school's safety officer happened to be walking by the classroom as the obscenity spewed out. The safety officer filled the doorway with his six-foot, five-inch frame and said, "Come with me."

Candrero knew he was leaving, but he wasn't going quietly. In his mind, he could hear his older brother's laughter. In one mental scene, his big brother laughed mockingly when he heard that Candrero left as soon as the safety officer ordered it. In another, the older brother laughed admiringly as he listened to Candrero tell how he resisted the safety officer. In the name of his pride, Candrero chose to play out the latter daydream; he folded his arms, puffed up all four-feet, nine inches of his pre-adolescent frame and said, "Make me." For emphasis, he punctuated his resistance with another obscenity.

The safety officer said, "One more chance. Come with me or I'll carry you."

Candrero sputtered another obscenity and added, "You can't touch me. I got rights." Then he swung his fist at the safety officer, who caught Candrero's arm before his fist connected.

Candrero shouted again, "You can't touch me. I got rights." He swung his other arm, and the safety officer caught that one too. The safety officer turned Candrero toward the hall. Candrero shouted again, "You can't touch me. I got rights."

Candrero continued yelling the same couplet as the safety officer steered him to the principal's office. While this scene guaranteed Candrero praise from his older brother and consolation from his mother, it also added another non-learning day to countless days spent in the principal's office or serving in-school suspension.

This scene plays out daily for too many students in Candrero's school and in schools everywhere. The example is common. This scenario seems like a ritual or a repetitive game with the students and adults locked in their roles. The students act out, and the adults react authoritatively and remove students from the classroom. After all, they must *keep school* from disruption. These rebellious students lose learning time every time they receive some kind of punishment. The adults believe that they are teaching school by preserving a quiet atmosphere for the other students, but clearly they are not serving students like Candrero.

Candrero and others like him who cry out that they "got rights" put an ironic stamp on this example. The irony lies in the fact that they do not have the right to disrupt classes. Even more tragic, one of the consequences for their disruption prevents them from exercising their right to learn. They are removed from class, and, beyond that initial consequence, they typically serve a punishment that limits their learning opportunities either in time-outs or in-school suspensions staffed by part-time or non-instructional staff or in out-of-school suspensions, with little or no teaching support. By the time the incident and its consequences end, these students may have lost at least an hour and perhaps up to a day or more of instruction. The adults may have *kept school* for all, but they have *taught school* only to some, excluding students with both academic and social education needs.

This scene should not be so common and predictable. Students should face consequences for their acts, but the consequences should educate them and change their social behavior and should never interfere with social or academic learning time.

The strategies in this chapter suggest ways that school leaders can stop the repetition of this scene. The *I-got-rights* game typically develops from several choices that adults make in the lives of children like Candrero. Such adults include any school personnel as well as parents and guardians. Collaborative school leaders need to help these adults make wiser choices to ensure that students really can exercise their rights to obtain a good education.

Strategy 6
Collaborative School Leaders Share Instructional Opportunities, Choices, and Wisdom

Studies from business and industry have indicated that any leader's psychological state influences everyone else in the organization. One might argue that school communities take on the characteristics of school leaders' personalities as well. Schools involve important relationships that are prerequisites to teaching and learning. If school leaders are healthy emotionally, they can lead a school community in establishing healthy relationships for collaboration in teaching and learning. School leaders' basic well-being enables them to share instructional opportunities, choices, and wisdom.

Such sharing is necessary because many students and their parents, as well as some teachers, do not have hope, do not know how to hope, and need to learn how to hope. Some of the rhetoric about school leaders' need to establish a shared vision refers to school leaders' ability to share hope about the opportunities that education in their schools provides to all students. However, school leaders have to acknowledge much about adults' prior experiences to teach them to hope.

U.S. census data indicate the depth of schooling's effect on the adult population. More than 10% of adults are high school dropouts, and that number varies in different regions of the United States. While reasons for dropping out of high school vary, an underlying factor may be poor relationships in the school community; that is, high school dropouts may have made such dismal choices because of their negative relationships with teachers, students, or other members of the school community.

Some of the negativity between high school students and their teachers develops because teaching and learning can become little more than a power struggle. Adolescents need opportunities to make some of their own choices in guided and safe situations. Lamentably, research on high school teacher–student relationships and instructional styles points to potential problems. Research shows that extreme teacher control alienates simultaneously maturing and rebellious adolescents. Other research on high schools and middle schools shows that if adolescents fail to develop a sense of belonging with both teachers and peers, they drop out.

Because young people have little sense of long-term consequences, they are not deterred from dropping out by a prognosis for poor employment and lifelong financial struggles. In fact, studies of the intergenerational links between dropouts who are very young parents and their teenagers show that parents' negative experiences with schooling can make it more likely that their teenagers will also fail in school and drop out.

School leaders are obligated to interrupt the dropout cycle, but dealing with the extreme negativity of at least 10% of the school community requires changing some conditions for the rest of the community as well. One of the many challenges to increasing student high school graduation rates is to change the power struggles between teachers and students as well as to involve parents or guardians and other adults who influence the students in the process of education. Many parents, even those who have graduated high school, hold deep resentments from their struggles for control with former teachers and school administrators.

School leaders must create an invitational environment that minimizes power struggles. School leaders must empower parents who have been alienated previously. Collaborative school leaders also need to teach teachers how to share power instead of trying to overcontrol all situations.

A school that invites parents, rather than summons them, extends a choice for participation. When parents have choices, then they are more empowered. The school leader sets the degree to which a school is invitational and welcoming. When a school leader invites a parent to school, but then overwhelms that parent with a roomful of educators, the parent likely feels ambushed.

Why would a school leader conduct an ambush? Some teachers may feel more secure in facing a parent with other teachers and the principal present. The principal is not afraid of the teachers and may understand the teachers' concerns about meeting the parent, a stranger, alone. The mere fact that parents are strangers to teachers and school leaders illustrates the divide between a welcoming school in which parents are collaborators with teachers and principals and the typical school where the lack of connection between educators and parents becomes the basis for many unfortunate conflicts. Because strangers do not trust one another, many parents and educators automatically distrust each other. The collaborative school leader must lower the distrust between each group.

Teachers may seem to have the most direct connection to parents because of their relationships with students. Yet the degree to which the teacher–student relationship is weak, which can be measured by the amount of student misbehavior in the classroom and in the halls, can influence the degree to which the teacher–parent relationship is weak.

Parents naturally hear more about school and any misbehavior from their children than from teachers or principals. In addition, students of any age are more likely to describe classroom disruptions than class lessons. As a result, students get the first chance at shaping parents' and guardians' perceptions about the school. The high likelihood that parents want to believe their children and to protect them merely adds to the strength of children's view of what happens at school. Therefore, when a teacher contacts a parent, his or her point of view may conflict with the mountain of images, accurate and inaccurate, sketched by the child. The teacher may need to overcome these images before resolving misbehavior or academic problems. Depending on the child's beliefs about the degree of strain between the teacher and student, the parent or guardian may resist any offers of partnerships with teachers or other school personnel. Students already have shaped parents' perceptions, and the typical teacher practice of calling parents as a last resort may be too late. In fact, because teachers wait for the last straw, they may reinforce the child's stories and thus the parent's suspicions about how bad the teacher may be.

Following their common mistake of contacting parents as a last resort, teachers typically also err by assuming they have all the answers to student deportment. Their goal may focus on obtaining the child's compliance in class (keeping school). Parents' goals, however, generally focus on learning (teaching school). What parents and guardians want to know is whether their child is as smart as other children.

Once the teacher plows into the particular problems with a child and how to fix them, parents often barely have time to understand the extent of the break in the teacher–student relationship. Teachers rarely help parents sort through each side of the issue: the child's and the teacher's. Before most parents can think about where to affix the blame, the teacher too often offers a plan to resolve the problem in a manner that will obtain what the teacher desires. Parents cannot support their children in the face of such a plan because they have too little information. They have arrived late in the situation, and their natural inclination is to resist the *mean* teacher about whom their child has griped. The probability that parents and guardians will resist teacher solutions dips even lower if a panel of school personnel faces them. Facing a group of educators who unanimously list a child's faults only increases a parent's wish to resist. With one teacher or a group, parents and guardians may feel cornered with no choices; that is the very definition of an ambush.

To avoid the chances of a future ambush, the principal must ensure that teachers establish relationships early with parents or guardians as well as with students. Teachers who greet parents as they drop off or pick up their students simply extend the little courtesies by which relationships begin. Teachers build better relationships when they call parents regularly just to chat and update the parents or guardians about classwork. These informal contacts build the trust that is necessary for parents to believe the teachers' views about their students' successes as well as disappointments or incidents. Principals too must be visible to offer those hellos and good-byes not only to students and parents, but also to all members of the community. Evidence of the warmth of a school comes from the greetings that all members of the school community extend to each other through such simple exchanges as asking after family members and former students. These courteous exchanges infiltrate classrooms and do not just linger in the hallways or parking lots.

Collaborative school leaders use informal moments to walk and talk with students and all the adults in their lives. Although some people push a formalized, so-called *professional* approach to colleagues and the school community, teachers and staff respond better to leaders who adapt to the language and customs of their school and its community. Community members appreciate leaders who speak their language, whether it is a form of colloquial English or a language other than English. When school leaders model an informal approach, they help teachers see how to build rapport with students and the communities where they live.

Sometimes teachers require a more direct approach to building community relationships. They need their collaborative school leader to do more than model a way to build relationships. Their school leader must set them specific tasks such as keeping logs of contacts with parents, including analyses of specific topics and the parents' reactions. Collaborative school leaders may need to require teachers to set and meet a ratio of positive-to-negative communications each grading period. Students do not change without the involvement of their parents and community. Education is change, and teachers cannot educate without support from their students' parents and community.

Education can liberate, but school rules and classroom instruction may be more oppressive than liberating in many schools. In an attempt to cope with school disruptions, some teachers create rigid boundaries in their classrooms. Using these rigid rules, they try to survive the turbulence of a chaotic school culture or poor neighborhood and school safety. Instead of creating a safety cell in their own rooms, they increase the conflict by battling chaos with rigidity. Teachers cannot change school security issues individually. They must unite and seek help from inside and outside the school to change from dangerous to safe conditions.

Collaborative school leaders point out the symptoms of and threats from poor school culture or safety and then ask all involved for help in changing the environment. Change is risky, and making a place safer involves reassuring and demonstrating to those involved that the changes will be better. Such a process is difficult because the immediate reaction to change is that things get worse before they get better. Wise collaborative leaders alert the community to the possibilities of negative as well as positive responses to change.

Because change is a process and the positive consequences lag behind the initial negative reaction, some students and parents may not experience the long-term benefits of the change. Collaborative school leaders must acknowledge this troublesome possibility to those students and parents. Realistically, changes start with one group of students and work to the benefit of others. Collaborative school leaders must solicit these individuals' investment in the future for the common good rather than for individual gain. The result of the investment may not be 100%, but open acknowledgement of each person's contributions will generate more support. Again, the little courtesies of thank you notes or any other local customs that express gratitude go a long way to sustaining a positive change. In contrast, failure to acknowledge openly the contributions toward change as well as the potential downside of change can generate a block of opposition.

Resistance to change is not only about an individual's failure to perceive personal benefits. Resistance also comes because those with control resent the collaborative leader's empowerment of others. The tools of resistance include gossip fueled by anecdotes and myths.

Strategy 7
Collaborative School Leaders Dispel Myths and Counter Gossip

Resistance to change draws from a knowledge base of local anecdotes, myths, and fables. Stories are potent means of persuasion. Generally, gossip is fueled by stories of disaster and impending doom. People repeat gossip that reveals the vulnerability of powerful people. Change is a challenge to everyone because every change shifts the balance of power.

In schools, the balance of power rests on intangibles. Some teachers possess power because of how long they have taught. Others, teachers and staff as well, possess power because of their prior personal, and perhaps intergenerational, connections to children and families. Alternatively, because of family ties, business connections, or allegiances to college and university alma maters or fraternal organizations, powerful people in the community endow some teachers and school staff with power. At the same time, some school staff cultivate school leaders and win a bit of immunity from school rules or more favorable access to scarce school resources. Some staff also gain power from their connections to extracurricular activities, or they generate power from popularity with students, parents, and guardians. Others establish financially based power through fund-raising connections with extracurricular clubs and activities. None of these power bases is inherently bad.

The problems arise when those with power make choices that do not represent the best interests of children. As everyone knows, the problem with power is that it can corrupt the people who hold it. Given these complicated and somewhat invisible sources of power in school communities, any change threatens established relationships and also threatens the people who hold power.

In reaction to a threat, gossip is the most potent weapon. Gossip spreads based on word-of-mouth connections, and the necessary networks for generating rumors are well established in these hidden bases of power. Accurate or not, each person in the hub of relationships that holds power can recall, or make up, extreme anecdotes regarding any shifts in the status quo. Each nexus in these power networks can generate a myth about the consequences of disturbing the current situation.

Collaborative school leaders have an understanding of the complex webs of power in their school communities. When they propose change, they must also be prepared to counter the threads of gossip that spin along these power grids. Collaborative school leaders use data as a tool for dismantling rumors, countering single-case anecdotes, and diffusing gossip.

Strategy 8

Collaborative School Leaders Use Data and Language to Share Experiences

Data can offset the power of anecdotes. Not surprisingly in the information age, educators have increasingly begun to use data as a teaching tool. In addition, data provide a mounting dictionary for education. Education that uses the language of data can shift stories from fantasy or individual experiences to shared experiences.

Given the potency of relationships in schooling, most educators focus their work on the reactions and schoolwork of individual children. Large class sizes may create a challenge to teachers because even though a class may have a group dynamic, grades and learning occur student by student. As a result, when teachers consider the degree of success in their work, they tend to think in moments. They tell stories about individual pupils rather than relate information about groups of students or certainly not about each group's overall performance. Most teachers' reflections about their teaching reveal stories of a particular student's successes or failures. Teachers rarely describe their work in terms of a group's performance on tests or summative data and statistics. These reflections about individual students may help enhance daily interactions, and they may show the strength of the teacher–students relationship that is so important to learning. On the other hand, such reflections easily convert to anecdotes about unusual situations and may not reflect the overall positive or negative experiences of pupils. Anecdotes, because they are stories, are retold, embellished, and eventually expand into a myth or rumor depending on the intent of the storyteller.

Data can serve as the counterbalance to potent anecdotes, rumors, and gossip. Data can provide a more balanced perspective on daily events, given that each school day may include at least one emotional event per classroom, if not more. Sometimes the emotional event includes many students, but it often rests on one pupil's or one parent/guardian's interpretation of a situation about which neither other students nor their teacher was aware. With a broader view of classroom events, teachers, students, and others can achieve a different perspective and interpretation of each situation. A careful review of accumulated data allows analysis of and reflection about students and their work in a broader context than reeling from one emotional story to another permits.

Collaborative school leaders balance emotional stories with a broader perspective. While individual stories must be respected, the collaborative school leader empowers each individual by sharing information that helps students, teachers, and parents review their situation in a broader context. Showing respect for individual performance while also monitoring the broader indicators of student and school performance requires collaborative school leaders to use language and data ethically.

Strategy 9

Collaborative School Leaders Are Principally Principled Teachers for Everyone

Ethical collaborative school leaders regard their role in schooling as consisting of ongoing teachable moments. To be collaborative, school leaders recognize that the lifelong processes of education apply to themselves (see the final chapter of this book, which dwells on the specific strategies that collaborative school leaders use to continue their learning). As lifelong learners, collaborative leaders accept a shifting balance of power in their interactions with teachers, staff, students, parents, and other community members.

Presuming formal preparation for their positions, collaborative school leaders recognize the teachable moments in their work. In such situations, school leaders discern when others offer insights and also when others seem adrift and lack information that they need. This delicate balance is achieved through self-awareness, sensitivity, and adherence to the fundamental ethics which ensure that their work provides a benefit for both the common good and the individuals involved. When conflicts between individual benefits and the common good arise, collaborative school leaders use knowledge and wisdom to achieve a balance and grow positive relationships.

Wisdom comes from understanding that relationships involve power sharing rather than power accumulation. An ethical approach to sharing power among members of the school community requires leaders to maintain principles that promote both the common good and individual welfare. To do this, collaborative school leaders do a lot of teaching to improve the relationships among members of the school community. At the very least, collaborative school leaders begin by attending to the fundamental condition of teacher–student relationships.

Strategy 10
Collaborative School Leaders Ensure Positive Teacher–Student Relationships

Many teachers and students need to be freed from repetitive power struggles. Teachers need to recognize and weather students' developmental issues in order to redirect and reteach students how to act, share, and participate in a community. Given their propensity to think about individual students and the distractions of emotional, yet momentary, incidents, teachers often lack enough background information to mitigate the intensity of some situational power struggles with their students.

In fact, some teachers have been inexpertly instructed not to seek background data on their students. Such misguided direction may have stemmed from an attempt to prevent teachers from stereotyping their students without meeting them or perhaps making biased rather than accurate instructional assessments of their students' present levels of performance. However, without adequate data concerning students' backgrounds, teachers may make unfounded assumptions that are equally as damaging to students as stereotypes.

Because teachers may not have studied the background information on their incoming students, they may lack the preparation as well as the resources for addressing their students' educational needs. Many teachers begin the school year in such a way that the data they possess for their classes of pupils may be literally a blank page in the grade book (Figure 2.1).

The image of a blank page does not help teachers plan instruction adequately or create good learning experiences. The blank-page image implies that all the teacher has to do is leave her mark on each student. Yet, realistically, teachers recognize that a lot of other people have already written on each student's page. Those people range from parents and family members to strangers and previous teachers.

Somewhere in the back of their minds, teachers remember U.S. Census summaries about the number of children living with single parents, divorced parents, or in poverty. Despite that recognition, teachers do not necessarily attach that information to their own students until there is some kind of event that requires parent contact. Until that critical incident, teachers may harbor a picture of childhood and parenthood that owes more to the fantasy of children as a blank page or the misrepresentation of real family life on television and in other popular cultural media than to the realities revealed by U.S. demographics.

Teachers need to acquire a realistic understanding of what their students bring to class before incidents arise. Collaborative school leaders help teachers find the regional data for their students and families from sources like the U.S. Census, Kids Count (from the Annie E. Casey Foundation), and other reports on childhood and family configurations. A school leader may need to remind teachers of the general facts about their students' lives and home environments in the school communities.

From such sources, the U.S. picture of childhood is more realistically attached to pupils in public schools. About 22% of families depend on the father's income only, or fit the popular description of a nuclear family. In fact, U.S. households are relatively small, including only slightly more than three people. While 50% of first marriages end in divorce, 60% of remarriages also end in divorce, and 54% of divorced women remarry. Seventy-five percent of white children live in two-parent homes, and 5% of white children live with a parent who never married. Among Hispanic families, 64% of children live with both parents, and 36% of African-American children live with both parents. About 29% of two-parent homes include college graduates. Among children younger than 18 years, 27% live in poverty, and 7% live in extreme poverty. About 60% of children live in families designated as working poor. Although many regions of the country no longer are predominantly white, the U.S. Census shows that 76% of the population is white, with 13% of African-American and 13% of Hispanic ethnicity. While these statistics have implications for all institutions in the United States, schools and teachers should heed the following numbers: 52% of households have no internet connection, 7% have no car, and 3% have no phone. When school leaders go over these numbers

Name	Homework Assignment #1	Homework Assignment #2	Homework Assignment #3	Quiz #1
Anikota				
Bradley				
Carla				
Dante				
Elise				
Frank				
Gayle				
Hiram III (Trase)				
Isabella				
Jonah				
Karen				
Larry				
MaLisa				
Nathanyel				
Olivia				
Paul				
Quarly				
Roger				
Serena				
Tiako				
Uma				
Vernon				
Wanda				
Xavier				
Yanie				

Figure 2.1. Beginning of the Year Blank Grade Book.

Project #1	Homework Assignment #4	Homework Assignment #5	Quiz #2	Test #1	Unit Average

Figure 2.1. *Columns continued.*

with teachers, they need to illustrate how these statistics can and will affect teaching and learning.

One way to help teachers work through the implications of national and local demographics is to associate the numbers to the way that they work. Instead of allowing teachers their gradebooks with a blank page at the beginning of the school year, school leaders should take the local figures and distribute them over a typical class in their school. Figure 2.2 provides a hypothetical overview of a typical classroom using national demographics.

As distributed in Figure 2.2, the overall numbers take on meaning. Teachers can literally see that many parents may be struggling economically because better than half of the class fits the designation of working poor. Instead of laboring over a misperception that pupils are merely careless about homework, teachers may see the many distractions to doing homework in households where everyone is working, perhaps even the student, or in households where the nonworking parent is also a dropout. Instead of frustration with parents who do not help their children with homework, teachers may find some compassion for a single mom who may be overwhelmed with the demands of work and parenting as well as confused by the complexity of the homework assignment.

Provided with a more realistic picture of the child's home life, the teacher may be more likely to recognize how "TV sitcom-inspired" expectations of formality, courtesy, and other expressions of respect may be different from what the child has experienced. Teachers often describe their frustration with students' poor behavior and exasperation that children do not act better with assertions such as "they ought to know better." Instead of expecting students to know already how to act in groups, teachers may recognize that students who do not have many siblings, or who may be home alone a great amount of time, may have experienced few chances to learn how to act in groups. Teachers may develop a deeper appreciation for why teaching students ways to work in groups is a part of their curriculum.

Teaching school focuses on developing students' academic and social growth. *Keeping school* simply enforces rules, which many students may have had no prior opportunities to learn.

The combination of background information associated with pupils' educational needs shown in Figure 2.2 can clarify the challenges for teaching and learning that the whole school community may face. Teachers may develop some insights into their students from viewing such a hypothetical table. Then, they should be encouraged to develop a background set of data on the students in their classes. Knowledge grounded in local demographics can help teachers develop reasonable expectations for student performance and give teachers better information on which to base their relationships with the students and their parents or guardians. Couldn't such background demographics change the school personnel's approach to such situations as the *I-got-rights* game with which this chapter started?

As much help as national and local demographics can provide in designing instruction for students, school leaders must recognize those among their staff members who cannot or will not learn to understand their students, their students' families, and the wider community. Such school personnel must be counseled to leave the profession or at least be removed from the school. Without a doubt, collaborative school leaders must have support from their own supervisors and central office or district personnel in removing or transferring such school personnel. While collaborative school leaders make every effort to support staff efforts to understand and instruct students, to provide a safe environment, and to develop positive community relationships, these school leaders do not hesitate to remove staff that cannot or will not make the changes that ensure a *good education* for every student. School leaders must know the abilities and disabilities of their own school staff.

Name	Gender	Race/ Ethnicity	Family Size	Family Housing Status	Family Head
Anikota	Girl	Na. Am./ Alaskan	3	Rent home	2 Parents
Bradley	Boy	White	2	Rent apt.	Single mom
Carla	Girl	White	5	Rent home	2 Adults
Dante	Boy	Afr. Am.	2	Housing proj.	Single mom
Elise	Girl	Hispanic	4	Rent home	2 Parents
Frank	Boy	White	2	Housing proj.	Single mom
Gayle	Girl	White	3	Own home	2 Parents
Hiram III (Trase)	Boy	White	3	Own home	2 Parents
Isabella	Girl	White	3	Own home	Single mom
Jonah	Boy	Mixed	4	Own home	2 Parents
Karen	Girl	White	2	Rent apt.	Single mom
Larry	Boy	White	2	Rent home	Single mom
MaLisa	Girl	Afr. Am.	3	Own home	2 Parents
Nathanyel	Boy	Afr. Am.	5	Rent apt.	Single mom
Olivia	Girl	Hispanic	2	Housing proj.	Single mom
Paul	Boy	White	3	Rent apt.	Single mom
Quarly	Girl	White	2	Rent apt.	1 Grandparent
Roger	Boy	White	2	Rent home	Single dad
Serena	Girl	White	3	Own home	Single dad
Tiako	Boy	Asian	3	Own home	2 Parents
Uma	Girl	White	3	Own home	2 Parents
Vernon	Boy	White	4	Rent home	2 Parents
Wanda	Girl	White	5	Rent home	2 Parents
Xavier	Boy	Hispanic	5	Own home	2 Parents
Yanie	Girl	White	3	Own home	2 Parents

Figure 2.2. Hypothetical Class with U.S. Census Demographics.

Parental Marital Status	Parental Educational Level	Parental Employment Status	Family Socioeconomic Status	Educational Needs
Married	HS grad.	1 Income	Working Poor	Math/no internet
Never married	College grad.	1 Income	Working poor	Gifted/underach.
Cohabit	HS grad.	Unempl.	Poverty	Spec ed.
Never married	Dropout	Unempl.	Extreme poverty	Spec ed./no car/ no phone
Married	HS grad.	1 Income	Working poor	No internet
Never married	HS grad	Child support	Poverty	No car/no internet
Married	College grad.	2 Income	Middle	
Remarried	College grad.	2 Income	Middle	Spec. ed./ no internet
Divorced	College grad.	Alimony	Poverty	Underachieving
Married	College grad.	2 Income	Middle	Science
Divorced	HS grad.	Alimony	Middle	No internet
Cohabit	HS grad.	Alimony	Poverty	No internet
Married	HS grad.	2 Income	Middle	Gifted
Divorced	Dropout	1 Income	Working poor	Spec. ed.
Never married	Dropout	Unempl.	Extreme Poverty	ESL/no internet
Cohabit	HS grad.	Alimony + 1 income	Working poor	No internet
Divorced	HS grad.	1 Income	Working poor	Underachieving/ no internet
Divorced	HS grad.	1 Income	Working poor	Underachieving/ no internet
Divorced	HS grad.	1 Income	Working poor	No internet
Married	College grad.	1 Income	Middle	Overachieving
Cohabit	HS grad.	1 Income	Working poor	
Cohabit	HS grad.	2 Income	Middle	
Cohabit	HS grad.	2 Income	Working poor	No internet
Married	Dropout	1 Income	Working poor	ESL/no internet
Remarried	HS grad.	2 Income	Working poor	No internet

Figure 2.2. *Columns continued.*

Strategy 11

Collaborative School Leaders Leverage Community Support for Students, Teachers, and Their Families

Students and their families are not the only part of the teaching-learning process reflected in community demographics. Teachers also face the same kinds of social challenges reflected in the U.S. Census statistics on family life. Teachers experience some of the same challenges with juggling child rearing and jobs as students and parents. School leaders need to understand and address the social issues of both students and teachers and other school personnel.

While collaborative school leaders can enlist help from teachers in identifying and addressing students' social needs, school leaders must carefully consider the social services that may be required among their staff members. Although certified staff (teachers and other licensed educators) may be held to higher social standards than the general public, the status of family life and marriage in the United States affects all members of the school staff, certified or classified, alike. Figure 2.3 distributes U.S. family demographics for a hypothetical school staff of 30 people.

Like students, the school staff lives in small households of about three people each. Unlike the general population, school staff members are college graduates with middle incomes. About 40% of U.S. teachers are under the age of 40 years. More of the school staff is white than is the student population. Almost 76% of public school educators are female, but school administrators are generally older white males. These demographic distributions offer insights into possible sources of conflict and need among school personnel. Issues of class, race, age, and gender hold powerful implications for interactions among school staff as well as between school staff and the general school community.

School leaders who learn the backgrounds of their staff along with background demographics for their students and local communities have better means of identifying and leveraging the kinds of social services that will support teaching and learning. Given a clear understanding of staff and student needs, school leaders can better serve their members and the greater community.

Students and their families require information and support for ensuring learning. Teachers and their families also need social supports for ensuring good teaching. Collaborative school leaders armed with local demographic information can identify those needs and seek better ways of shoring up the services that can lead to better home lives and good school conditions for staff and students.

School leaders use local demographics to find the social service resources that are available in their communities. Once they identify the pertinent issues, they need to discover where not-for-profit groups, community organizations, and governmental agencies fit into the school community. Armed with census information about their students' and teachers' backgrounds and needs, school leaders can approach the agencies, organizations, and groups for help with their particular needs. Many businesses try to offer services to schools, but are rebuffed. Sometimes these volunteers are turned away because of concerns about student safety, but school leaders who reach out to law enforcement agencies can address such concerns. However, most of the time, schools cannot afford to turn away offers of local support. When school leaders hold facts about their students' and staff's needs, then appropriate partnerships can be arranged among schools and their communities. Collaborative school leaders promote collaboration between schools and other entities.

Name	Gender	Race/Ethnicity	Age	Family Size	Family Housing Status
Andy	Male	African Am.	24	1	Rent apt.
Betty	Female	White	38	3	Rent apt.
Carla	Female	Hispanic	35	5	Own home
Danita	Female	White	33	4	Own home
Elvira	Female	White	45	2	Rent home
Fred	Male	White	32	3	Own home
Gloria	Female	African Am.	47	5	Own home
Hannah	Female	White	40	4	Rent apt.
Ida	Female	White	54	1	Rent apt.
Janet	Female	White	43	6	Own home
Katherine	Female	White	51	2	Own home
Laura	Female	White	22	1	Rent apt.
Mike	Male	White	30	2	Rent apt.
Nelson	Male	White	61	4	Own home
Octavia	Female	White	55	2	Own home
Pauline	Female	African Am.	26	3	Parents' home
Qootah	Female	Asian	23	1	Rent apt.
Ruth	Female	White	25	4	Rent apt.
Stan	Male	White	43	5	Own home
Tara	Female	White	49	2	Rent apt.
Uteah	Female	Native Am.	26	5	Rent home
Veronica	Female	White	41	2	Rent apt.
Wallace	Male	White	43	2	Rent apt.
Lance	Male	White	44	1	Rent apt.
Yvonne	Female	White	45	4	Own home
Ann	Female	White	56	4	Own home
Benita	Female	White	45	5	Own home
Charles	Male	White	43	4	Own home
Dorothy	Female	White	46	4	Own home
Ellen	Female	White	40	3	Rent home

Figure 2.3. Hypothetical Staff with U.S. Census Demographics.

Family Head	Marital Status	Educational Level	Position
Self	Never married	Bachelors	PE/coach
Single mom	Divorced	Masters	Aide
2 Parent	Married	Masters	ESL teacher
Single mom	Separated	Bachelors	Classroom tchr.
2 Adults	Cohabit	Masters	Art tchr.
2 Parent	Married	Bachelors	Computer
Single mom	Divorced	Masters	Classroom tchr.
Single mom	Separated	Masters	Counselor
Self	Never married	Bachelors	Classroom tchr.
2 Parent	Remarried	Bachelors	Spec. ed.
2 Adults	Remarried	Masters	Spec. ed.
Self	Never married	Bachelors	Classroom tchr.
2 Adults	Cohabit	Masters	Counselor
2 Adults	Remarried	Doctorate	Principal
2 Parent	Married	Masters	Asst. principal
2 Parent	Never Married	Masters	Classroom tchr.
Self	Never Married	Masters	Music
4 Adults	Never married	Bachelors	Classroom tchr.
2 Parent	Remarried	Bachelors	Classroom tchr.
2 Adults	Never married	Bachelors	Classroom tchr.
Single mom	Never married	Bachelors	PE/coach
2 Adults	Divorced	Masters	Spec ed.
2 Adults	Married	Masters	Reading
Self	Divorced	Bachelors	Classroom tchr.
2 Parent	Married	Masters	Classroom tchr.
2 Parent	Married	Masters	Classroom tchr.
Single mom	Remarried	Masters	Librarian
Single dad	Divorced	Masters	Science
Single mom	Remarried	Bachelors	Classroom tchr.
Single mom	Divorced	Masters	Classroom tchr.

Figure 2.3. *Columns continued.*

Summary

Instructional leadership focuses on student achievement and discipline. Collaborative school leaders with their mission for *teaching school* rather than *keeping school* are instructional leaders. They recognize the teachable moments in every aspect of school and community life. They regularly review school data such as discipline and achievement records to monitor the learning environment. They also review background data on teachers and students as well as the school community to identify community strengths and weaknesses. Collaborative school leaders work to focus their communities' resources, efforts, and services on improving learning and social conditions for students and teachers through the following six strategies.

Strategy 6—Collaborative School Leaders Share Instructional Opportunities, Choices, and Wisdom

- They practice emotional health in order to lead the school community to social healthiness.
- They look for opportunities to help all students and staff learn.
- They understand that learning includes addressing developmental issues of self-discipline and self-control for all students, staff, and families.
- They work to mediate student, teacher, and family power and control issues.
- They exercise wisdom in leading teachers to develop positive school–family relationships.

Strategy 7—Collaborative School Leaders Dispel Myths and Counter Gossip

- They help teachers and students focus on success stories.
- They counteract community stories of disappointment and failure with accurate information and data.

Strategy 8—Collaborative School Leaders Use Data and Language to Share Experiences

- They use school and community data to create a shared understanding of student needs.
- They counterbalance anecdotes and rumors by supplying a broad and data-based perspective on student achievement and needs.

Strategy 9—Collaborative School Leaders Are Principally Principled Teachers for Everyone

- They understand that all adults in the school community face as many learning and development issues as the students.
- They view school events and issues as opportunities to teach staff, families, and communities how to better serve the student body.
- They share power to promote both the common good and individual welfare.

Strategy 10—Collaborative School Leaders Ensure Positive Teacher–Student Relationships

- They monitor the school community and school environment for a positive approach to learning, social development, and social service needs that lessen power struggles.
- They help teachers understand that their students are more complicated than blank pages.
- They use local census data to guide staff to a realistic understanding of student, family, and community needs.
- They hold teachers accountable for addressing student needs.

Strategy 11—Collaborative School Leaders Leverage Community Support for Students, Teachers and Their Families

- They monitor local census and social services data on the status of families, the economy, and other measures of community well-being.
- They understand the implications of the local census information for supporting teachers and other staff in their work.

Chapter 3

School Culture and Community

Strategies 12 through 14 for Collaborative School Leaders

12. Collaborative School Leaders Monitor the Environment

13. Collaborative School Leaders Maintain the Health of the Environment

14. Collaborative School Leaders Honor a Student-Centered Culture over an Adult-Centered Culture

The internal school culture can be supportive of student learning, or it can merely make the adults very comfortable. Collaborative school leaders strive to increase student learning, and although they care about their staff's needs, serving the staff does not mean merely making the school comfortable for adults at work. While good relationships among the staff can make learning better, schools often serve only the adults and ignore the students. This chapter includes three strategies that help collaborative school leaders maintain an intense focus on learning.

Strategy 12
Collaborative School Leaders Monitor the Environment

Collaborative school leaders keep an ecological view of the school's culture and climate. An ecological view means that the school's culture and climate includes all physical and psychological systems. So from the soap dispensers in the restrooms to the feelings of the student who just lost a relative, to a teacher with a cancer diagnosis, to the instructional aide whose boyfriend gave her a black eye, to the science club's bake sale, the school leader must develop some systematic and regular methods for keeping track of these important details.

Many school leaders have a network of informants who tip off the principal to a variety of incidents, but as useful as these informants try to be, their information may be biased. More dangerously, their tidbits often are sporadic and unsystematic.

For something as fundamental as soap dispensers, the school leader works out a regular routine for a member of the staff to maintain them. Collaborative school leaders encourage all of the other members of the school community to alert that staff member to any soap needs. Sometimes staff members find ways to buffer themselves from routine requests, and sometimes students use soap information for avoiding the routine of attending class. So the school leader must make sure that those buffers are removed and that routines are upheld.

One example of resistance to routines includes teachers' failure to maintain or turn in school records. Many teachers fail to understand the ways that administrative routines ensure safety and improve the school's environment. In fact, some teachers may see these routine requests as oppressive. The following vignette illustrates the way that a teacher's omission in routine not only disrupted the school, but also poisoned the culture and climate of the school.

Nice Day to Go to the Track

The brilliant spring day's bright blue sky surrounded puffy white clouds that seemed to spell "hooky" for all the middle school's staff and students. The guidance counselor passed the principal in the hall and said, "I can't find Ms. Askipahid's class." The principal glanced in the direction of the fifth grade hallway and frowned. Although the fifth grade had joined the middle school last fall, the transition to a fifth through eighth grade middle school moved seamlessly from the sixth through eighth grade configuration of the past decade. The fifth grade hallway abutted the sixth graders, but the schedules had worked to ensure few opportunities for fifth and sixth graders to clog the halls or literally bump into each other. Although some fifth graders and their parents had worried a lot about the move to the middle school, the teachers had worked to calm their fears, and the guidance counselor reported that her checks with those students and families showed a growing level of comfort with the middle school's team approach. The principal simply could not imagine how a teacher and class could disappear.

"Pardon me, but what?" the principal asked.

The guidance counselor responded, "I don't want to alarm you, but Ms. Askipahid's class isn't in its room. I've just come from the media center, and she's not there and neither is her class."

The principal asked, "Is she and the class in another of the fifth grade rooms?"

The guidance counselor shook her head no. "I checked that before the media center. I was headed to the cafeteria."

The principal turned on his walkie-talkie and contacted the office. "Ms. Lopez, was Ms. Askipahid's class supposed to go on a field trip?"

The walkie-talkie squawked, "No, but maybe you need to come here."

The principal and guidance counselor exchanged looks. Such a request indicated that Ms. Lopez had something to say that she did not want broadcast over the walkie-talkie. They strode quickly to the office.

Ms. Lopez met them near the back of the reception area and led them into the principal's office. "I heard Mr. Teller say something about Ms. Askipahid mentioning what a nice day it was and then something about going to the track. And I remember all this because I have not been able to find her for 15 minutes. I have a mom waiting in the office to take her child, who is in Ms. Askipahid's class right now, to the orthodontist. This was merely embarrassing for the first 5 minutes, but now I'm worried."

"What track? The ball field?" the principal asked.

"I have no idea," Ms. Lopez answered.

"What if it's the race track!" the guidance counselor mused. "I suppose they could walk." Investors and race fans had built a new speedway about a mile and a half from the middle school, and today was opening day. Races were to start at 1:00 PM. The time was 1:25 PM.

"Oh, for Pete's Sake!" the principal sputtered. She picked up the phone and dialed the assistant principal. "Paul, could you take a walk around the building and over to the ball field. Ms. Askipahid and her class aren't in the building. She didn't mention to anyone where she was going. And one of the parents is here to pick up her kid who is in the class." She hung up the phone and said, "I'll drive around the school grounds and over to the speedway." She grabbed her keys and headed to the parking lot.

Halfway to the speedway, the principal's walkie-talkie crackled. The assistant principal's voice called out, "I've found them. They were headed back from the track at the ball field."

The principal responded, "Ok. Tell Ms. A. that I'll see her in my office at the end of the day."

The assistant principal replied, "Already told her that."

After student dismissal, Ms. Askipahid sat across from the principal and smiled. She started speaking in a rush. "It was such a lovely day that I just couldn't keep the students cooped up in the classroom. I took them out to let them run on the track. And we did some math about distance. When Paul caught up to us, we were using what we'd figured out about distance on the track to calculate the distance from the track to our classroom. I think it's a great way to learn, and I'd do it again because they seemed to enjoy it so much!"

The principal responded, "Why didn't you let anyone know that you were going to do this?"

"Well, I'm the teacher, and I get to decide what's best for my students."

The principal asked, "Did you know that one of your students' mothers was waiting to take him to his orthodontist's appointment? Did you know that they were late and not only had to reschedule, but also were charged for missing an appointment, a visit they didn't have? Can you imagine how upset that mother is? Do you want to pay her for the cost of missing that appointment?"

Ms. Askipahid shook her head, but defiantly responded, "Well, they shouldn't make voluntary health appointments during the school day. I've seem the letters you've sent advising parents not to do that."

"I can advise, but I can't change the fact that some orthodontia isn't voluntary and sometimes appointments are very hard to get. Besides that, any parent should have confidence in finding their children anywhere at this school within minutes— not a half hour later. I still want to know why you didn't tell anyone where you were going with that class." The principal slowly stated each word of the last statement for emphasis.

The teacher looked at her hands in her lap. "I still believe I acted within my professional judgment about my class. I'm a professional, not an hourly worker."

The principal lowered her voice, "You're a professional under my supervision and employed by the school district; you are not an independent professional. The terms of your employment are that you follow this district's judgment and policies about what to teach, when, and where to teach it. I review your lesson plans to make sure you are doing that, and I come into your classroom to see what you are doing. Given all of this, you didn't act within your professional judgment because you didn't follow any district or school rules about you or the students leaving the scheduled place for your class."

Ms. Askipahid frowned. "That's exactly why I didn't tell you. I knew you'd say 'no' or put up so many picky bureaucratic obstacles that I couldn't just seize a teachable moment and go!"

The principal sighed and said, "Ms. Askipahid, you may have made a teachable moment out of the trip to the track. However, I think this trip is teaching more about you than the students. Usually teachable moments arise out of students' experiences and actions; this incident arose from you. In addition, by not telling anyone where you were going, by not planning this trip, you raise all kinds of questions about what you have accomplished. Did the students learn more than they might have by staying in the classroom? I believe they enjoyed it, but where is your evidence of learning—what you intended for them to learn and what they learned?"

The principal paused, but went on before Ms. Askipahid could form an answer. "From a set of safety issues, do you know how many students in your class have allergies? Among those who do, which one might have had an attack while you were out there? How would you have received help for that student or anyone who might have received some kind of injury? What if the mother who came for her child had come because of an emergency? What do you think a delay of half an hour in finding her child might have meant in an emergency?"

Ms. Askipahid turned her palms up and shrugged, "What do you want me to do?"

The principal answered, "I'd prefer that you plan these kinds of outdoor excursions in advance, but I realize that the weather plays a role in whether or not you can do this. So you could make an outdoor lesson for use in good weather and then, when you have the opportunity to use it, just notify the office of where you'll be. We will give you one of the office walkie-talkies so that you can call back for help or we can notify you if a parent has come."

Ms. Askipahid looked puzzled. "You mean, you would let me take them outside on short notice?"

The principal laughed and replied, "You would have planned for the short notice. That's the difference."

The teacher still looked surprised and a little confused. "You'd give me a walkie-talkie?"

"Of course. We need to make sure that you and the students are safe and reachable at all times. It's not that you should always teach in one spot and never vary from that regimentation. You just need to work with the rest of us in making sure that students are safe and learning something."

Schooling should not be a dismally regimented experience for student or teachers, but the sheer number of people in one building requires systematic ways of ensuring everyone's safety and ability to learn. Collaborative school leaders must find a balance to protect students while enabling teachers to seize teachable moments. Just as students need to learn social skills, teachers need to learn how to negotiate their *academic freedom*.

Some teachers hijack schools from a focus on students through abuse of academic freedom. *Academic freedom* combines two complex terms and creates another term that can also confuse people. *Academic* is an often-used term to indicate irrelevant and/or highly abstract ideas with little practical meaning. However, the term *academic* also can refer to strict processes of reasoning and analysis used to develop knowledge and understanding. The word *freedom* often signals lack of restrictions, but in our system of government, each freedom comes with responsibilities attached.

Academic freedom refers to a teacher's right to practice responsible instruction about rigorously developed knowledge without fear of arbitrary reactions. Academic freedom gives teachers the right to teach responsibly for their employers, the school district. However, some teachers believe that academic freedom means that they have no restrictions at all.

Teachers employed by school districts have many restrictions. They must have a license to teach, and that license carries with it ethical obligations. Their employer, the school district, can place more restrictions on the teachers as an exchange for paying a salary. In many states, the state legislature place restrictions on what courses and curricula districts must offer, and those restrictions are passed on to teachers. Every layer of restrictions enhances the meaning of *academic freedom*. Teachers must meet those restrictions as their responsibility and obligation in the first step to their protection under *academic freedom*. Some teachers think they can shield themselves from the state's or district's restrictions by hiding behind academic freedom. In other words, a kindergarten teacher may state the belief that she shouldn't teach reading to 5-year-old children because they are too young, but if her school, district, and state all promote a curriculum of reading for 5 year olds, she has to teach that curriculum. She cannot hide behind academic freedom and refuse to teach what her contract specifies she must.

School leaders must help such teachers recognize their obligations while also allowing them to voice their professional concerns. A collaborative school leader would permit the concerned kindergarten teacher to submit her evidence of how reading instruction isn't suitable for 5-year-old students. In this case, the teacher would have difficulty generating that evidence. Considerable research shows how reading skills are formed very early in life. Nevertheless, for many years, some kindergarten teachers widely held the belief that such instruction was harmful. By aiding teachers to find the appropriate evidence to support their beliefs, the collaborative school leader helps the teachers maintain their professional confidence and gives them some professional development at the same time. Academic freedom permits teachers to speak out, but they also must meet their contractual and professional obligations first.

Teachers are not the only members of the school community who need help understanding school routines and rules.

Strategy 13

Collaborative School Leaders Maintain the Health of the Environment

Collaborative school leaders monitor routines and periodically help staff members, parents, students, and community members remember why the routines help them. Many people chafe at rules and do not understand why rules are necessary. Collaborative school leaders explain and teach the benefits of those rules. For many parents of elementary students, school rules seem overwhelming and do not fit their ideas of how much fun their young child should have at school. For those parents, collaborative school leaders explain that the more people included in a group, the more rules are necessary to help the group work. Even families of two (e.g., one adult and one child) have rules such as "Knock before entering the bathroom" or "Pick up your own mess," and other rules designed to help the two people get along better.

Collaborative leaders know that words make a difference. Sometimes it helps people to think of rules as agreements about getting along with each other. Many people experience punishment from the enforcement of rules. In contrast, they realize that agreements mean a bargain, where they get something when they give up something else. Collaborative leaders know their environment well enough to choose a vocabulary to help them explain their schools' and students' needs to other people.

Strategy 14

Collaborative School Leaders Honor a Student-Centered Culture over an Adult-Centered Culture

In many schools, teachers stay in the same classroom year after year and the students do not. Every year, students adjust to new classrooms, different teachers, a different schedule, a new locker, and a different lock combination, along with other personal changes in height, weight, and body shape. Students face continual change.

In contrast, the adults spend a lot of time on time. They make a schedule and stick to it. They schedule the day and the classes. They schedule performances and meetings. Once they set the times for courses, they set a calendar for events in the year ranging from sports to concerts. That means they set schedules for spaces and building use. They worry about the amount of time students take to learn something. In short, the teachers struggle with issues of time management.

School leaders must recognize the different challenges faced by the teachers and students—time and change, respectively. Collaborative school leaders make the students' issues the focus of the school. Teachers' issues are important to the degree that those issues affect students. Collaborative school leaders must guard against all the ways that teachers' issues can dominate and even suppress the students' needs.

School leaders grapple with issues that have more in common with teachers' issues. Their time, too, is fragmented, interrupted, and a constant source of worry. In addition, school leaders know the teachers better than the students because the students change every year. Because identifying with the teachers comes so easily, collaborative school leaders must consciously force themselves to concentrate on student issues and always remember the fundamental question about all school activities, discussions, and issues: How does this benefit the students? Collaborative leaders use that central question to guard against creating an adult-centered school environment.

The following vignette illustrates how the school leader focuses on students, not on adults.

Math in the Morning

For 15 years, Colossalian Elementary School scheduled art in the last part of the day for its first graders. Because 6-year-olds need help with coats and mittens during the wintertime, the first graders' art class lost 30 minutes to getting ready for dismissal. The art teacher asked if the first grade class could switch with the fourth grade class. Fourth graders could manage to get ready to dismiss in less time than the first graders. The first grade teachers were appalled at this idea because the fourth grade art class met as soon as school started. The first grade teachers expressed concern that if the first graders had art when school started then their reading class would come at the very last part of the day.

Most first grade teachers prefer to teach reading at the beginning of the day. The principal pointed out that the teachers did not have to trade the art schedule for the reading slot. Instead, they could move art to the beginning of the day and slide each subject's schedule down the list. This suggestion, however, horrified the first grade teachers almost as much because that meant the math class moved to after lunch.

The principal asked, "Ok, why is math after lunch bad?"

The first grade teachers rattled off several answers.

"Math is as important as reading and has to be done in the morning when we're all fresh."

"We've always done it in the morning."

"My planning period shifts with this new schedule, so I'll have to get all the math materials together at lunch time."

"If I have lunch recess duty, then I'll be too hot and sweaty or cold and frozen to be able to teach math."

"I'm so tired after lunch."

"That's the low point of the day for me too. I've always filled the hour between lunch and art with social studies and science. Stuff that's easy to do or cut short when they aren't paying attention."

The principal held up his hand. "So far, you haven't told me how math in the afternoon hurts the students, just you."

One of the teachers replied, "You mean if we can show you how students are affected by changing to math in the afternoon, you'll change it back?"

The principal answered, "We'll figure out something else if math in the afternoon causes the students not to do as well on tests or other aspects. What kinds of evidence would you use to show how students benefit or do not benefit from math in the afternoon?"

"We have their math scores from kindergarten last year."

"We could compare how well last year's morning math group did with how well the afternoon math students do."

"We could just count how many fall asleep and take little after-lunch naps," quipped one of the teachers.

"We could do that now," chimed in another, causing everyone to laugh.

By repeating his question about the benefits to students, this principal gained the focus that he wanted. He moved the group from anxious complaining about adult concerns to a workable action research project with a focus on students' learning.

Schools need to be student-friendly places. While many teachers will tell you they want to teach because they like children or the subject matter, and many will state that they teach because they like to learn, those reasons are not enough to make schools student-friendly.

Other reasons for teaching make it even less likely that schools will be student-centered. Many teachers do not like students in general, only certain students who share their subject matter interest or who are very compliant in their dealings with the teacher. Some teachers find that they prefer their own children to working with other peoples' children. Study after study shows that most teachers choose the profession because they believe that schools offer a convenient schedule for their family life. These teachers may become resentful because teaching requires more time than just the hours spent with students. That resentment may spill into relationships with students.

Taken together, these adult concerns combine to make schools more adult-oriented than student-focused.

Collaborative leaders have to help adults rise above their own needs and grievances to create a focus on the students. Teachers and other staff must appreciate the students and their needs. *Appreciate* means to be aware of, admire, be sensitive to, and respect. It does not mean love, like, or revere, although any of those emotions and actions can make appreciation of students easier.

Some adults can learn to appreciate students and their needs, problems, behavior, and development. Other adults are too self-involved to appreciate students at all. The latter group pushes to make schools spaces for adults rather than students. Collaborative school leaders must guard against such shifts in focus and even occasionally remove self-involved adults from the schools in order to keep the focus centered on what is best for students.

Confusion surrounding the word *professionalism* can also interfere with the central purpose of education—to serve the needs of students. Most of our society holds professions in some regard. Doctors and lawyers may not experience the esteem held in past generations, but people certainly envy their social status. Most people recognize that professionals must be well educated and paid accordingly.

Teachers often believe that a professional approach is a desirable approach. Unfortunately, many studies of the perceptions about schools held by parents, guardians, and the community show poor reactions among the very people teachers might hope to impress with their professionalism. Teachers may dress with care to appear professional, but some community members may feel intimidated or even angered by attire that emphasizes differences in social class. Many teachers write careful, formal letters to parents or guardians, but the parents or guardians report that such letters seem cold and unwelcoming to them.

These reactions may perplex some teachers, but others learn that they can hide behind their professionalism and avoid working with anyone outside of their classrooms. Collaborative school leaders need to step in and address these problems with professionalism. In what ways does professionalism benefit students? Even under the best of circumstances, that question is tough to answer. Collaborative school leaders can replicate, for their own schools, the studies that reveal negative reactions to so-called *professional* practices. Such materials can provide teachers direct evidence about the school community's perceptions of them and increase their awareness of the so-called *professional* practices that alienate parents and others.

Parents also carry their own distractions from students' needs. Under the best of circumstances, parents can be their children's best advocates. Many parents, however, who want to be their child's advocate do not have the skills. Some parents simply avoid the responsibilities of child-rearing and want teachers or the principal to take care of their children's needs without bothering them. Other parents want a say in every aspect of their children's day. Schools face a range of parent needs and abilities; individual schools must be responsive to the particular mix of parental needs and abilities in their own communities.

Collaborative school leaders try to determine the extent and variety of parental needs so that students' learning improves. They use teachers' parent-contact logs, participation in conferences with parents, and informal conversations with parents in the community or at school events to measure what parental needs might be. They also directly ask parents what kinds of needs they have. For example, middle school parents may talk about their worries about drugs, sex, or peer pressures. Elementary and secondary parents may reveal concerns about violence in the community and gangs.

Collaborative school leaders know that relieving these parents' worries will improve students' learning. Their response to worries about drugs, sex, and peer pressure may include video tapes, meetings with counselors, or discussion sessions for parents about these topics. Their response to violence and gang issues includes enlisting community watch information and setting up sessions with local law enforcement. Collaborative school leaders even take risky steps such as meeting with gang members and discussing ways to make schools a safe place.

Some parents, guardians, and family members carry burdens that displace their attention to the children. These individuals have drug, alcohol, or other physical and mental health issues that place more attention on themselves than on their children. Collaborative school leaders find ways of addressing those social issues so that the focus can revert to the students. They reach out to social services or law enforcement to protect the students.

Some families do not hold the same views as the rest of the school community. Although their children attend the school, these families seem to challenge the teachers' instruction continually. Collaborative school leaders set up alternatives, but they also support teachers who are instructing as required by their employers. Teachers may resist developing alternatives for such families, but a democratic education requires choices and options. Once alternatives are provided, families can choose to participate in one alternative or another. If the family refuses to pick an alternative, then the school leader may invite them to make other arrangements for their children's schooling. Collaborative schools leaders recognize irreconcilable differences.

Parent organizations always claim their purposes as support for students and the school. However, some parent groups boost parents more than the students or the school. Collaborative school leaders negotiate a clear focus on students with those groups. If necessary, they ask for audits of funds raised in the name of the school. They implement safeguards on the parent groups to make sure that students benefit first.

School leaders refuse to let members of the public hijack the school for purposes other than students' benefit. With an aging population, many schools reside in communities where as much as 90% of the public have no children in school. Collaborative school leaders find ways to make that 90% care about the school's students so that they feel connected to students' successes. Collaborative school leaders find both formal and informal groups in the public with whom they can talk about their students' abilities and needs. For example, a collaborative school leader may make a point of talking about students' musical talents and then schedule the students to perform at a mall or nursing home. By exposing students to the public in ways that highlight student achievements, collaborative school leaders can help adults accept the need for schools as well as the investment in helping schools. Displaying students' abilities also lowers public gossip, rumors, or misconceptions about the quality of children perpetuated by various media.

Finally, collaborative school leaders cultivate media relations. Members of the media have their own professional norms that do not focus on what is best for students. For most journalists, the purpose of writing a story is more about building their résumés than about addressing any social or personal issues for any child or group of children. Even though the collaborative school leader remains aware of the media representative's motives, he or she can direct that reporter to stories that lead to better outcomes for the students.

Summary

Good schools revolve around their students. Students' learning fills the core of any good schools' events, schedules, and routines. Collaborative school leaders insert student concerns into every activity, every consideration, and every conversation with anyone about their schools. They always use strategies designed to achieve a goal that answers the main question: How does this benefit students? This chapter introduced three strategies for collaborative leaders to use in helping everyone involved in education to focus on answering that one critical question about the benefit to students.

Strategy 12—Collaborative School Leaders Monitor the Environment

- They establish routines for regularly monitoring and renewing the physical environment.
- They use a systematic approach to ensure that every student and staff member is in the right place at the most optimal time for learning.
- They help teachers negotiate academic freedom to meet students' needs while respecting differences in community members' expectations for student learning.

Strategy 13—Collaborative School Leaders Maintain the Health of the Environment

- They help teachers recognize ways in which the routines or environment needs to change to support student learning.
- They help families understand how and why groups need routines and rules to support student learning.

Strategy 14—Collaborative School Leaders Honor a Student-Centered Culture over an Adult-Centered Culture

- They understand that staff issues are important to the degree that those issues affect students.
- They remain advocates for students despite their natural inclination to identify with adult matters.
- They encourage staff and families to appreciate all students in all of their needs and diversity.
- They hold other educational professionals accountable to the ethics and obligations of the profession.
- They cultivate the larger community's interest in the students' accomplishments and well-being.

Chapter 4
Administrivia

Strategies 15 through 18 for Collaborative School Leaders

15. Collaborative School Leaders Delegate and Check
16. Collaborative School Leaders Follow the Owner's Manual for Regular Maintenance
17. Collaborative School Leaders Recognize the Sound of a Smoothly Running Engine
18. Collaborative School Leaders Set Goals and Monitor Indicators

In the current press for educational accountability, principals and many others express concern about the scope of responsibilities in school leadership. They stress the difficulties of heightening their attention to instruction while also fulfilling the substantial number of routine matters that eat up a leader's time and energy. These worriers make an important point; instructional leadership requires a foundation of school safety and cleanliness along with well-designed and well-managed school schedules and budgets. Despite their concern about the scope of the work, the problem for these school leaders is not the addition of instructional leadership accountability on top of management requirements; their major problem stems from one of the scarcest resources among all school shortages, time.

Time management provides the basis for all the strategies recommended in this chapter. Although students, teachers, staff, parents, and other community members form an unpredictable mass of human behavior, school leaders can reasonably expect to tackle any unexpected events within carefully implemented daily routines and schedules.

Too often, poorly managed schools treat time casually. Such schools leap into crisis mode for traditional activities, as if these events were unexpected episodes. For example, if the school has an annual banquet for student athletes every June, that date should be on the school's calendar in September. The coordinator for the annual banquet should assume responsibilities from the previous coordinator at the banquet in June. The principal should not have to cast around for so-called *volunteers* to coordinate the banquet in September or December, and certainly not in May. These poorly managed schools wear out staff and volunteers because of the constant drama of rallying to cover every poorly planned event. While school personnel are in a state of overdrive, students can take advantage of the chaos and of their frazzled nerves. When schools mismanage time, they sow the seeds of failure for student achievement.

Every school leader must budget time with as much or more care than any other school resource, including money. The school leader must budget scare time to the development of instructional materials and school schedules, to the formation and activities of school committees, and to the supervision of instruction and students.

Even though no school would buy textbooks without reviewing their contents and making a cost-benefit analysis, schools rarely calculate time costs of such texts. How much time does it take teachers to learn how to use the texts? How much time does it take to prepare student materials before a lesson? How much time does it take to distribute student materials during the lesson? How much time will teachers or students spend retrieving and storing the materials? When totaled, how much does each of these expenditures of time eat into a lesson? Does the failure to calculate the time-costs connected to instructional materials undermine the instruction? You bet it does.

Although school schedules bedevil school leaders from year to year, some leaders focus too much attention on the details of a master schedule and forget to factor in annual events that disrupt the master schedule. Schools can lose instructional time to assemblies, professional development days, holidays, and fire or other safety drills. Without considering the monthly calendars of scheduled interruptions to school days, without planning a cushion of time for unexpected episodes such as snow days, school leaders and teachers may find a habitual, but preventable, loss of instructional time.

Imagine a block schedule in which courses meet on Mondays, Wednesdays, and alternate Fridays or on Tuesdays, Thursdays, and alternate Fridays. Given holiday schedules, the Monday, Wednesday, and alternate Friday courses stand a high probability of losing at least six to twelve Mondays in a 36-week school year. Then throw in the misfortune of professional development Fridays, spring break, one assembly, six pep rallies, and several bad weather days. As a result, the Monday, Wednesday, and alternate Friday schedule accumulates so much lost time that those classes might offer as much as 25% to 30% less instructional time than the Tuesday, Thursday, and alternate Friday classes. School leaders can prevent such instructional time losses by aligning the daily schedule with the annual events and then adjusting the schedule to balance instructional time across the curriculum.

Similarly, when school leaders establish committees to work on school issues, the school leader must make estimates that balance the available committee meeting time with the complexity of the issue. As an example, picture a school that establishes a committee to evaluate the school's discipline plan. The committee membership includes both parents and teachers. The school leader recognizes that the membership has time constraints. Most parent members cannot meet until the evening, but they also have to get home to feed their children, supervise their homework, and put them to bed. To complicate matters, most teachers resent working on any committee many hours past their contracted instructional day. Probably neither group will meet willingly over the weekend. All these constraints on time leave about two hours per evening meeting.

The committee may agree to schedule meetings once a month, but only during the school year, not the summer months. The agreement to meet monthly during the school year allots a mere 18 hours for this committee to work. Once the school leader recognizes the total time available to the committee, then he or she can specify the tasks for each hour of each meeting, and from that specification, the school leader can determine how likely it is that the committee will complete its evaluation of the school discipline plan in one school year. With this reasonable estimate of the committee's time and probable use of it, it is less likely that people will complain about whether this committee is doing anything or gripe that the committee is taking too long. From the beginning of its meetings, the committee will have a reasonable understanding of how much time they have to accomplish specific tasks.

Many incidents distract school leaders from paying attention to instructional leadership tasks. Because school leaders fail to budget time for instructional leadership, they consume scarce moments with discipline or maintenance issues. School leaders may record meetings with parents, vendors, or lunch duty in their date books, but they rarely block out time for classroom visits and observations. When they do not budget the time for instructional leadership, they do not get to spend time doing it.

This chapter describes several strategies that ensure successful management of such functions as maintenance, school routines, budgets, and other seemingly less important matters than teaching and learning. However, every strategy requires conscious awareness and careful attention to conservation of schools' most precious resource: time.

Strategy 15
Collaborative School Leaders Delegate and Check

Collaboration incorporates the strengths and weaknesses of all involved parties. A collaborative school leader seizes opportunities to encourage further development among the people with whom he or she works. Sometimes people need to refine a strength or to develop strategies to compensate for a weakness. Collaborative school leaders help the people with whom they work to make realistic self-assessments and then provide them with opportunities to address their strengths and weaknesses.

When collaborative school leaders delegate specific tasks with reasonable time lines, they provide others the opportunities for further development. Collaborative school leaders negotiate the specificity of tasks and deadlines as an accommodation to the developmental needs of each person. In every case, the collaborative school leader monitors people's progress in meeting the details and deadlines of these tasks.

Strategy 16
Collaborative School Leaders Follow the Owner's Manual for Regular Maintenance

Laws, courts, policies, and expectations rule schools. Collaborative school leaders maintain their knowledge of relevant laws, court decisions, state regulations, district policies, and their school communities' expectations. These various rules perform a similar function as a guide to a school leader's work as the owner's manual performs as a guide to the long-term use and maintenance of a vehicle. The number of visits new car owners must make to maintain their wheels may seem overwhelming, but failing to make those visits often proves more costly in terms of money and aggravation.

Just as a newly licensed teacher may inappropriately exercise academic freedom to overthrow the teacher's manual or the district's curriculum, some newly certified principals mistakenly try to improvise their responses to incidents. They reason that their professional judgment should count for something given the time and money they spent on graduate level courses and professional examinations in obtaining their license to practice school administration. Legally, they are not reasonable at all.

Most school incidents fit into some common category of human behavior covered by district policy or by civil, state, or federal law. School leaders must know those legal entities and jurisdictions by heart. New school leaders must look up nearly everything at first. Fortunately, many districts and most states have converted education law and policies to some electronic format, which is much friendlier to busy school personnel than hard copy notebooks or legal texts once were. The click of a mouse leads school personnel to specific instructions on fulfilling school, district, and state policies or laws pertaining to schools in nearly every situation.

In summary, laws, regulations, and policies script much of school leadership. These guides mean that most school leaders do not have to make up responses as they go through busy days full of unpredictable moments. Instead, school leaders can focus their energies on the unique issues, the truly odd moments, and let the routine matters settle as prescribed. Collaborative school leaders have the wisdom to recognize the difference between the predictable quirks of human behavior for which legal protocols already spell consequences and those purely unpredictable matters. Collaborative school leaders save their time and energy for wildly unique matters.

Strategy 17

Collaborative School Leaders Recognize the Sound of a Smoothly Running Engine

Silence can be as much a signal of something wrong as something right. Mothers can tell the difference in an infant's hungry wail and the crying sounds the baby makes when she's cold or wet. Collaborative school leaders know their schools well enough to recognize the signals that something is not working as it should.

Given the people-rich environment at schools, much of what school leaders must decipher rests in body language, rumors, and interactions with students, staff, and community members. Collaborative school leaders are sensitive to the moods and personality traits of the people in their schools. They strive to maintain the common courtesies of greeting people and inquiring about health and family as a genuine means of testing the health of the school community. These courtesies do more than symbolically smooth social activity; they offer information that signals the emotional and mental health of each individual. Some people serve as sensitive indicators that relationships may be strained or of individual stresses that lead to group anxieties. Collaborative school leaders carefully survey the people around them for signs that the school is doing well or that a problem may be simmering somewhere.

While collaborative school leaders attend to the qualitative signs that maintain a healthy school, they also develop more systematic, quantitative indicators of school health. Given the current era of accountability, many school leaders collect quantitative data to comply with state or federal requirements. Because their schools may not have had a systematic information system prior to these requirements, these school leaders may spend too much time on collecting information that is minimally informative about a school's health. Collaborative school leaders set up information systems that monitor the business of their schools from student achievement to attendance to budgets.

While collaborative school leaders ensure the security of these databases, they also use industry standards for relational data analysis software. These leaders use reliable statistical analyses to explore data about instruction and management systems to spot trends that can signal student or faculty strengths and weakness.

By exploring their schools' databases and the relationships among the data, collaborative school leaders seek potential problems. Problem-finding may strike some people as a form of buying trouble, but bigger trouble finds schools whenever school leaders try to avoid problems instead of seeking them.

Collaborative school leaders need to recognize the reactions of anger and disbelief that sharing some data can produce. People commonly avoid bad news, especially if the data show something that differs from their personal experiences or awareness. Evaluators term this kind of avoidance *data denial*. School leaders also suffer from data denial.

Don't Tell Me, I Don't Want To Hear It

An experienced principal, Anne Maricha, built her reputation on turning around two low-performing schools. She first made her mark as a teacher leader in a school where 88% of the students participated in federal free and reduced-price meals. She worked with teachers to adopt instructional methods that depended heavily on measuring student learning through classroom assessments on each part of the curriculum. Students' grades rose from these data-based strategies. Moreover, the state-mandated test scores in that school soared, and the district tapped Ms. Maricha for her first principalship immediately after she obtained her certification.

As principal of another low-performing school where the majority of students lived in poverty, 25% were also homeless, and the school enrollment changed as much as 78% in a year, Ms. Maricha also achieved high test scores. In that school, Maricha included a data-based approach to monitoring and changing student learning and discipline. By monitoring both sets of data, Ms. Maricha and the teachers changed some of the school rules as well as addressed some of the students' poor social skills to create a calm school where students learned. Again, Ms. Maricha's data-based approach increased students' scores on the state-mandated tests. The district awarded Ms. Maricha's success as principal of this school by assigning her to Mattelin High School.

Mattelin High School's teachers and parents expressed concerns that their school's fine reputation suffered from declining test scores and a change in the school community. MHS once had been noted as a good example of a comprehensive high school, but for nearly 15 years, changes slowly eroded MHS's status in the district. Some of the changes included changes in neighborhood attendance patterns. As MHS's immediate neighborhood aged, with fewer residents who had school-aged children, students traveled more and more by bus from streets miles away from MHS. Many of those areas housed lower-income families than MHS's immediate neighbors. At least one of the far-flung areas included several social service agencies, a homeless shelter, and a shelter for victims of domestic abuse. A mental health agency also erected a building to serve long- and short-term juvenile mental health patients. These students attended MHS sporadically, some enrolled for merely days and others for months at a time.

While the average number of poverty-level students at the school was low, those students who lived in poverty faced extreme conditions, and the students who were not living in poverty reflected extreme affluence. When plotted on a graph, the demographics of family socioeconomic status at MHS resembled a bowl rather than a bell curve. MHS did not have a middle class.

These extremes shaped parent and community involvement as well. Typically, the affluent parents created events suited to their social circles, and, either deliberately or with callous oversight, they did not invite the parents, guardians, or family members of students from poorer neighborhoods. Not surprisingly, the affluent families' voices dominated the school. These families pushed for programs for gifted students, but resisted any notion that some of the poorer students possessed any gifts or talents. Despite an abundance of special programs for gifted students, the school's test scores continued to steadily decline. Many of the teachers agreed with the outspoken parents who blamed the "social service kids," especially the transient students from the mental health group home—never mind that this organization never enrolled more than eight students at a time. Their presence singly and collectively disrupted halls, the cafeteria, and some classes such as physical education. The commotion generated by any one of these students provoked constant parental complaints about imagined dangers to their child or children.

MHS went through two principals in 18 months, one of whom complained that the affluent parents' micromanagement of every aspect of the school drove him away. The district superintendent, under pressure from a school board member, contacted Ms. Maricha. Maricha considered the offer an opportunity to demonstrate that her data-based approach might work under any socioeconomic conditions since her previous successes came in schools known for serving children in poverty. MHS parents and staff seemed to appreciate her systematic no nonsense approach. They welcomed Ms. Maricha and demanded that she apply her data-based approach to improving their school.

Ms. Maricha surveyed the available information system at MHS. She was pleased to note that through the influence of MHS's affluent parents, the school had state-of-the-art administrative hardware and software as well as well-established databases on students, their grades, and attendance. Maricha felt confident that these conditions would make her task much more efficient. Rather than enlisting a few staff members to help her gather, key-in, and clean data, as she had to do at her previous schools, she could immediately begin the necessary trend analyses that parents and staff claimed they needed. All it would take at MHS was a few clicks of the mouse, and the charts and graphs would be ready for everyone to discuss.

Because the school modeled itself as a traditional, comprehensive high school, Maricha reported data disaggregated by grade level and subject area for groups of students. She also disaggregated data by subject area departments, such as math, English, social studies, and the sciences. She compiled the information in plenty of time for presentation on MHS's "Data Day." The planned events included her presentation to faculty in the afternoon and then another to share the compiled analyses with parents in the evening.

On Data Day, teachers eagerly paged through the students' by-grade-level and by-subject-area tables of grades and discipline infractions. However, the faculty's mood darkened when they turned to the by-department reports of grade distribution and discipline referrals.

One of the veteran and most instructionally innovative science teachers, with a reputation for rebelliousness, blurted out, "What the hell is this crap?"

A long-time friend of the outraged teacher, the biology teacher, who frequently tried to soften her friend's comments, this time snapped, "Well, sure looks like our new principal is out to make the students' problems the teachers' problems. And these charts make our department look like it has more problems than anyone else."

Ms. Maricha spent the rest of the meeting defending her methods of extracting and analyzing data. Members of the Science Department engaged in petty arguments about data fields and missing data using vocabulary that bewildered the rest of the faculty, although Maricha thought she held her own position well.

Nevertheless, Ms. Maricha felt very alone in her attempts to explain what trends she saw in the charts and tables. The moment she mentioned talking to parents about the reports, the Science Department gained unanimous support. The rest of the faculty erupted in a hubbub of protests that forbade Ms. Maricha from distributing any of the information to parents. From the Art Department to the Science Department, the teachers argued a variety of objections to providing information to parents. They accused Ms. Maricha of exposing them to community ridicule and perhaps even violence based on her charts about discipline referrals from particular departments as well as data on which department gave more As or Fs than the others.

Unfortunately for the faculty, an instructional aide, who was also a parent, was present. She spoke in favor of other parents receiving the data. The faculty interrupted her comments repeatedly, but she persisted. She argued that parents had a right to understand what the trends in the school were. When the faculty tried to argue that departmental information amounted to personnel issues that were supposed to remain confidential, she reasonably responded that no individual teacher information appeared in the charts. She insisted that confidentiality rested only in individual teacher files. Her winning point was that even if Ms. Maricha did not distribute the charts and graphs to parents, the aide could make copies available. Several faculty members walked out of the room in a huff, and Ms. Maricha dismissed the rest. She met with the parents and gave them their copies of data reports that evening as planned.

This incident escalated into a yearlong battle with the faculty on one side of any issue and parents on the other supporting Ms. Maricha. Maricha could never broach the faculty's resistance, and the district sent Ms. Maricha back to the classroom at the end of the school year.

Maricha applied for principal positions outside the district and found a school where she spent more time including others in the data collection and analysis process before she distributed results. Ms. Maricha learned the hard way that delegation of some of the data processing permitted more buy-in and provoked less denial of the results than her ill-fated assumption of the entire task.

Strategy 18

Collaborative School Leaders Set Goals and Monitor Indicators

Beyond the common response of data denial, the preceding example illustrates that sometimes collaboration is learned in the process of developing as a school leader. Ms. Maricha developed into a collaborative school leader because she continued learning, and she set goals and monitored her own learning with the same systematic data skills that she applied to schools, students, and staff. Most federal and state accountability laws require schools to set or meet goals. School leaders may choose merely to comply with the goals established for their schools, or they may be more proactive.

Proactive approaches include establishing goals that may be steps to achieving more than accountability goals. Collaborative school leaders poll students, staff, parents, guardians, and communities to identify their desires and expectations for the school. Then with help from all, they translate those expectations into step-by-step sets of goals.

Using these steps, collaborative school leaders then develop measures to indicate how close or distant their schools are from achieving the goals. Monitoring includes finding baselines that help show growth. These measures are not simple checklists of whether or not people worked hard on tasks listed for achieving the goals. The measures include school data on attendance, discipline referrals, grades, test results, teacher performance and practices, and other genuine markers of change in a school.

Most of these markers will include the many basic functions of schools from cleanliness to social courtesies with which collaborative school leaders remain in touch. Management functions are not add-ons to the pressures of instructional leadership.

For many years, critics chided school leaders for any singular obsessive focus on administrivia. Instead, they argued that principals should ignore the management aspects of schooling and focus on instruction. Others argue today that the job is too big for one person and insist on separating management from instruction.

Collaborative school leaders recognize the interconnected nature of school management and instructional leadership. Instructional leaders need the fundamental management tools of data systems, fiscal management, control of the budget, safety, and building maintenance. Collaborative leaders also start by gaining control of the scarcest resource of schools: time.

Summary

This chapter illustrated how management and instructional leadership are interdependent. Smoothly running school operations permit a healthy learning environment. Collaborative school leaders use four strategies for ensuring that schools run smoothly for the interest and betterment of student achievement.

Strategy 15—Collaborative School Leaders Delegate and Check

- They budget and manage time.
- They provide staff with opportunities to participate in school operations.
- They give staff support and training for those opportunities.
- They monitor and check the results of staff's use of those opportunities.

Strategy 16—Collaborative School Leaders Follow the Owner's Manual for Regular Maintenance

- They know law, regulations, policies, and school rules.
- They know how to find out more about any law, regulation, policy, and school rule of which they may be unsure in any given situation.
- They apply law, regulations, policies, and school rules appropriately.

Strategy 17—Collaborative School Leaders Recognize the Sound of a Smoothly Running Engine

- They remain sensitive to qualitative indicators of students', staff's, and families' sense of well-being, good relationships, and a positive learning environment.
- They use systematic and quantitative indicators of school health including such databases as attendance, discipline, budgets, grades, achievement scores, and more.
- They work on preparing the community to recognize the signs of school performance and overcome community resistance to systematic school data.

Strategy 18—Collaborative School Leaders Set Goals and Monitor Indicators

- They solicit expectations about students' learning and development from students, families, teachers, staff, and community.
- They help the school community come to a consensus on school goals.
- They set indicators and timelines for steps toward achieving school goals.
- They regularly monitor indicators and meet timelines in reporting to the school community about the degree of progress toward goals.

Chapter 5

Attending to the Health and Welfare of Collaborative Leaders

Strategies 19 through 20 for Collaborative School Leaders

19. Collaborative School Leaders Maintain Their Physical Health
20. Collaborative School Leaders Maintain Their Mental Health

Throughout this book, the discussion of each strategy notes the simmering conflicts within and surrounding schools. Each chapter as well as every section alludes to the many ways that conflict swirls around school leaders. Most of the strategies listed in this book will generate conflict over issues that bubble beneath the surface, or lull people into believing that no issues exist. Although the public may generally acknowledge that school leadership encompasses a great deal of responsibility, and although they may realize that serious responsibilities also generate stress, most of the time, members of the school community do not recognize the signs that their school leader may be stressed, or even traumatized.

Many ingredients contribute to this general lack of awareness about school leaders' stress and trauma. For many, the very notion that a powerful person could suffer seems silly. Their view seems to be that power wards off all of the consequences of stress or trauma. Along with that general view of the benefits of power, school leaders themselves often deny that they suffer in their roles. Their denial of stress and trauma comes from a belief that they cannot admit any weaknesses or they will lose their position and power. Related to school leaders' denial comes another element in the cover-up of school leaders' experiences with stress and trauma. That element includes both the preparation and professional development of school leaders. Many professional development and preparation programs for school leaders prescribe resolutions to conflict that use avoidance tactics and/or suggest that stress and trauma result from serious personal flaws such as poor human relations or management skills. A few programs now admit the political practices surrounding school leadership, but fail to address the stressful aspects of political activities. Taken together, these influences may mean that school leaders do not develop the physical or mental health habits that they need to provide the wisdom or the focus on students that is essential to the success of every school community.

Strategy 19

Collaborative School Leaders Maintain Their Physical Health

No medical studies focus exclusively on school leaders' health issues. However, where any group of school administrators gather, tales emerge describing bouts with high blood pressure, weight problems, and other physical symptoms of stress. School leaders' problems with physical health may be an occupational hazard. One obvious step on the road to poor physical health includes not eating regular, balanced meals. And the failure to get adequate exercise represents another physical health hazard for school leaders. Both of these problems reveal common poor health practices among educators.

Schoolteachers are notorious for not eating their lunches or taking a personal break. Early in the history of public schools, one teacher and one room to a school meant that the teacher was constantly on call. While the teacher supervised breaks for the students, no one could cover for the teacher when she took a break. With larger multi-classroom schools, the situation did not improve much.

The federal Free and Reduced Price Meal Program arose from a now legendary story of the thousands of teachers who packed lunch for themselves, but regularly distributed it to needy students instead of eating it. Not until the 1970s with the advent of teacher unions did the teacher workforce earn planning periods and duty-free breaks, including lunch. Despite these provisions, many teachers still do not eat lunch because their planning periods do not coincide with the slots of time they use to clean up, change materials, and otherwise prepare for the after lunch lessons.

While school leaders may have learned to fill their lunch breaks with work as teachers, most schoolwide schedules encourage administrators to skip lunch. Because teachers supposedly enjoy a duty-free lunch break, administrators stand in as students' supervisors during lunch. Most schools permit students a relatively unstructured lunch period, which allows them to interact freely. Those interactions require supervision, however. Principals, assistant principals, and guidance counselors often spend chunks of their days either directly supervising student lunches or dealing with disciplinary issues that arise during the lunch period. Sometimes the only time available for meetings with working parents occurs during their lunch hours. For many school leaders, meetings or supervisory and disciplinary duties prevent them from experiencing a duty-free lunch. Missing lunch can lead to overeating at the end of the day or snacking on inappropriate foods during the day.

Just as overeating in the form of binging or snacking leads to obesity and a chain of related health problems, failure to exercise worsens physical deterioration compounded by stress. Many school personnel fail to get enough exercise. The school leaders' days include not only instructional hours, but also after-school activities like sports, student performances, and meetings. Recent studies of principals' use of time show that many arrive at school around 6 AM and stay through 10 PM, a 14-hour day. Within these 14 hours, principals may have skipped breakfast, lunch, and dinner without a moment to attend to their physical needs. Inserting a regular regimen of exercise into this jam-packed day seems impossible.

As described in the preceding chapters, collaborative school leaders must apply their creativity to every aspect of schooling. Certainly, they need to be creative to squeeze 20 or 30 minutes for exercise out of their nonstop days. Some creative ideas include walking a route near the school with students who walk to and from school. Such a walking trail not only provides exercise, but also opens an opportunity to get to know the school's neighbors. At first, the neighbors may acknowledge the principal with a mere wave or a curious stare. In time, the neighbors will approach him or her with conversations, ideas, and concerns. The exercise walk becomes not only a health asset, but also an asset to building school and community relationships.

Another creative way to embed exercise into a collaborative leader's day is to take various teachers for walks during their planning or lunch breaks. As noted above, teachers neglect their physical health to meet the demands of preparing lessons in their tightly-timed days. By pulling a teacher or group aside to walk the perimeter of the school, gym, or neighborhood, a collaborative school leader can set up an opportunity for informal bonding. As with the neighborhood walk, the teacher walk yields more than health benefits for the collaborative school leader. These walks encourage informal discussions and can lead to innovative approaches to school issues. At the very least, the discussions create a stronger partnership among school leaders and teachers.

Physical problems diminish a person's ability to think clearly or work well with few mistakes. All school personnel need their wits about them because of the demanding pace of schooling. The preceding 18 strategies require collaborative school leaders to think deeply, analytically, and strategically. The most basic steps to physical health include eating right and getting regular exercise. Collaborative school leaders must maintain their physical health to ensure their mental acuity.

Strategy 20

Collaborative School Leaders Maintain Their Mental Health

Periodic surveys report consistently that school leaders find their jobs very stressful. Mental health experts relate stress to a number of physical health issues as well as a group of mental illnesses that can vary in severity.

A few recent studies show that school leaders can be susceptible to trauma syndrome. These studies reveal a variety of verbal as well as physical assaults that routinely victimize school administrators. The educational leadership community, both academic and professional, resists the idea that school leaders, who hold considerable power, can be victims. Nevertheless, these studies provide a glimpse into the mental health issues that must be addressed to secure good mental health for school leaders.

Some of the symptoms of trauma include repeatedly reliving the events, an inability to concentrate on anything else, sleeping too much or too little, loss of appetite or overeating, depression, anxiety, and suicidal thoughts. Even though no systematic studies deal with the incidence of trauma among school leaders, every convention or meeting of school leaders offers war stories with examples of each of these trauma symptoms. The most obvious and common symptom is the repeated reliving of these traumatic events. Sadly, the term *war stories* among both professors and practitioners in the field of educational leadership merely indicates a disdain for these repeated tales. This disdain is unfortunate because by marginalizing these stories, the field misses an opportunity to deal with the trauma these tellings and retellings signify.

Because conflict is a working condition for school leaders, they cannot avoid the trauma of physical or verbal assaults. Collaborative school leaders must develop mental health strategies for coping with trauma when it occurs. First, they must understand that the trauma stems from forces larger than they or their power can control.

For example, a parent, guardian, or other member of the community who shouts obscenities at the collaborative school leader means harm to whatever that person imagines about the leader's office or role. The verbal assault is personal, but the leader must recognize the larger pressures represented by the shouting person. By removing the personal element, leaders separate their personal identities from their jobs. In other words, these leaders see the shouter as yelling at the job, role, or position, not them. When they make that mental separation between the object of the yelling and themselves, these leaders can respond more calmly to the upset person. More importantly, they can move into the next conversation without an overdose of leftover defensive adrenaline affecting the next person.

Naturally, safety comes first. Collaborative school leaders must recognize when they are, or are not, effective in calming the situation. Fortunately, a number of programs now provide both physical and verbal safety training for school leaders. Collaborative school leaders take advantage of such training and make sure that others in their school do so as well. They also create signals to other school personnel as to whether they need help. These signals can range from code words indicating a need for another person to come to their aid to an alert to summon school security or local police.

Even though some of these assaults seem random, something the school leader does or fails to do may trigger such assaults. Collaborative school leaders systematically determine what they do, or don't do, that starts these problems. Systematic reflection includes such practices as writing journals or undergoing behavioral analysis.

By writing in a journal, the collaborative leader keeps a diary of all contacts, such as phone logs, e-mails, letters, memos, and notes on face-to-face meetings and encounters. These journals include a date, time, and place with summaries of the ideas expressed and exchanged. To review the journal to figure out the effects of his or her behavior, the collaborative school leader methodically analyzes the journal entries relevant to the traumatic events. He or she looks for patterns. Did these events transpire on the same day of the week, such as every Tuesday? Did they occur at a certain time of day such as early in the morning or right after school? Were the events always in the cafeteria or at a certain spot in the hallways or office? Do these patterns fit any physical highs or lows for the school leader, or are they a signal of physical highs or lows for the other party?

Sometimes journals do not give the collaborative leader any insights into the causes of such assaults. Journals represent the school leader's perspective on events. All of us have blind spots in our perceptions about our own actions.

When journals do not help identify what the school leader did, or failed to do, to set off verbal or physical assaults, then a behavioral analysis can be useful. Modeled on the analysis of children's problem behavior, the school leader asks for a systematic behavioral analysis from a school psychologist, special education personnel, school guidance counselor, or other professional trained in these techniques. The professional records the school leader's words and actions in various settings on several days. The professional then analyzes the recorded behaviors to identify how the school leader may have triggered negative responses from other people. Together, the professional and the collaborative school leader can develop ways of minimizing the triggers that lead to such negative reactions from other people.

While systematic analysis of one's practices helps the school leader to cope with trauma, mental health in school leadership also involves diminishing more routine stress. As noted above, part of the strategy to deal with stress calls for good physical health habits. In addition to regular exercise and good diet approaches, collaborative school leaders need some strong mental health habits.

One of the strongest approaches to professional mental health habits entails making connections with other collaborative school leaders. Although many preservice and inservice programs advise administrators to join professional organizations, they often fail to explain the benefits of such groups. Along with other more tangible resources such as newsletters, conferences, or updates, these groups provide the mental health benefits of a network of support related to work. In most schools, the administrators practice their role alone. It is lonely at the top. Legal, educational, and ethical restrictions involving confidentiality isolate school leaders even more. Many studies show the mental deterioration that isolation produces. Collaborative school leaders recognize the dangers of "living in their own heads." They reach out to professional organizations or form support groups where they get regular reality checks from other people who face the same job stress.

Collaborative school leaders make another important step toward maintaining mental health by enjoying activities beyond their work. Although 14-hour days leave little leisure time, spending a half-hour on some hobby, reading a book, gardening, or even singing in the shower can lift a person's mood. A collaborative school leader can combine these mental health benefits by joining a community or church group or club that shares these interests. In contrast to the professional organization, these other groups can improve school leaders' mental health by distracting them from the constant minutia and turmoil of schooling.

Discussions of school leaders' physical and mental health rarely appear in educational leadership books. This omission comes about because of entrenched beliefs about leaders, power, and schools shared by school personnel and the public. Among these beliefs is one about the nurturing aspects of school personnel: principals are supposed to help everyone else; no one else needs to help the principal. This thinking sets up the school leaders for an unrealistic approach to their physical and mental health. Disillusionment with the extent of the work looms large among the responses of school leaders to the many surveys about stress in positions of school leadership.

Perhaps that disillusionment stems from the failure within the field of educational leadership to acknowledge and address the issues of physical health and mental health. Without question, school leadership takes a lot of time and requires high energy and stamina. However, the job is not too hard for everyone, but it may be too hard for just anyone. School leaders need to collaborate with others to benefit their mental and physical health as much as they need to collaborate to obtain a good education for students.

Summary

The fact that school communities reflect competing expectations about and interpretations of the definition of a *good education* for any and all students provides a peek at the constant conflict surrounding schools. Collaborative school leaders work in the midst of such conflict. Their central role places their physical and mental health at risk. This chapter offered two strategies for the maintenance of school leaders' health.

Strategy 19—Collaborative School Leaders Maintain Their Physical Health

- They monitor their health.
- They eat nutritiously and regularly.
- They exercise regularly.
- They attend to the staff and students' health in addressing their physical health.

Strategy 20—Collaborative School Leaders Maintain Their Mental Health

- They monitor their mental health for stress or signs of trauma.
- They learn strategies for de-escalating verbally or physically abusive people.
- They give themselves reality checks by using journals or consulting with trained personnel about the effects of their behavior on others.
- They consult with others in similar positions through networks.
- They enjoy activities outside of school such as hobbies or social groups who share their interests.